Happy 58th Bi[...]
Hope this h[...]"
    Lots of love,
        Pam + Alex xx

Praise for
GOLF FOR
ENLIGHTENMENT

✳

'An ethereal and delightful experience. Those of us who live in the game are often teased by what appears to be its specious nature. However, it is the genuine nature of what the game offers that is the very allure of this lovely book.'

—JEFF JOHNSON, PGA Professional

'Deepak Chopra has applied many of his teachings about life to the wonderful game of golf. I not only learned something about my approach to the game, but I learned how to apply these lessons so that I am able to focus my energies more efficiently in business. This is a "must read" for any executive.'

—KEN GUNSBERGER,
Senior Vice President of Morgan Stanley

'Just as we can't control many variables in the game of life, the game of golf also contains many variables we can't control. This book is a beautiful illustration of that, and shows us that many wonderful things can happen when we let go of that need for control.'

—KENNETH N. MAY, CEO and President of RCI

'The game of life and the game of golf are similar in that we put way too much emphasis on results instead of what we learn from the experience. This book is a wonderful reminder that the game of life and the game of golf are both a journey, and that journey is much more important than the destination.'

—LINDA REBROVICK,
Chief Marketing Officer of KPMG Consulting

'*Golf for Enlightenment* is a unique, entertaining, and thought-provoking book. The book utilizes a man's quest to conquer the game of golf by inadvertently teaching him how to see life in a different perspective. As with the game, it is apparent that Deepak Chopra's lessons in life will take years of constant practice to master. Yet along the way your enjoyment of the game will improve immensely, as will, perhaps, your game itself.'

—TOM WILSON, PGA Professional and Tournament
Director of the PGA Tour's Buick Invitational

'The literary equivalent of "hitting it on the screws." Chopra makes you step back to examine the fact that your life and your game are one and the same.'

—JOHN FRICKE, television and radio sports analyst

'This is not only a game plan for golf, but more importantly a game plan for life. Talk about a valuable "yardage book"! Deepak Chopra has molded and created something the Royal & Ancient never dreamed of. It's as if Chopra came back from the long session with Old Tom Morris. We are all the better for it.'

—EDDIE WHITE, Vice President of Team Properties for Reebok

GOLF FOR ENLIGHTENMENT

*

ALSO BY DEEPAK CHOPRA

*

Creating Health

Return of the Rishi

Quantum Healing

Perfect Health

Unconditional Life

Ageless Body, Timeless Mind

Journey into Healing

Creating Affluence

Perfect Weight

Restful Sleep

The Seven Spiritual Laws of Success

The Return of Merlin

Boundless Energy

Perfect Digestion

The Way of the Wizard

Overcoming Addictions

Raid on the Inarticulate

The Path of Love

The Seven Spiritual Laws for Parents

The Love Poems of Rumi
(edited by Deepak Chopra; translated by Deepak Chopra and Fereydoun Kia)

Healing the Heart

Everyday Immortality

The Lords of the Light

On the Shores of Eternity

How to Know God

The Soul in Love

The Chopra Center

Herbal Handbook
(with coauthor David Simon)

Grow Younger, Live Longer
(with coauthor David Simon)

The Deeper Wound

GOLF FOR ENLIGHTENMENT

The Seven Lessons for
the Game of Life

DEEPAK CHOPRA

RIDER
LONDON · SYDNEY · AUCKLAND · JOHANNESBURG

5 7 9 10 8 6 4

First published in 2003 by Harmony Books,
an imprint of Crown Publishing Group,
Random House Inc., USA.
This edition published in 2003 by Rider,
an imprint of Ebury Press, Random House,
20 Vauxhall Bridge Road, London SW1V 2SA
www.randomhouse.co.uk

Random House Australia (Pty) Limited
20 Alfred Street, Milsons Point, Sydney,
New South Wales 2061, Australia

Random House New Zealand Limited
18 Poland Road, Glenfield,
Auckland 10, New Zealand

Random House South Africa (Pty) Limited
Endulini, 5A Jubilee Road,
Parktown 2193, South Africa

The Random House Group Limited Reg. No. 954009

DESIGN BY LYNNE AMFT

Papers used by Rider are natural, recyclable products made from wood grown in sustainable forests.

Printed and bound by Mackays of Chatham plc, Chatham, Kent

A CIP catalogue record for this book
is available from the British Library

ISBN 1844130347

To my father, Krishan, who inspired me to play
   the game of life,
and my brother Sanjiv, who showed me that the
   game of life is mirrored in the game of golf.

Love,
DEEPAK

Acknowledgments

My deepest appreciation and thanks to my friends and family: Wendy Werley and Tina Mickelson for becoming part of my golf team through a series of synchronistic events. Wendy, thank you for being my instructor. Tina, thank you for your wisdom and insight.

Herb Moore, director of golf and general manager, and his staff at the Meadows Del Mar Golf Club in Del Mar, California, for making me feel at home.

John Steinbach, John Crisci, Will Miele, and Bob Maggiore at the TaylorMade-adidas Golf Company for their help in fitting me properly in all my golf equipment. I love my clubs!

Rita and Mallika Chopra, Candice Chen, and Baby T for supporting our family's passion for golf.

Sumant Mandal, Gotham Chopra, Sanjiv Chopra, Amit Anand, and Michael Bullock for being my supportive and patient golf buddies.

Ray Chambers, Tom Barrack, and José Busquets for sharing my passion with me "South of the Border."

ACKNOWLEDGMENTS

Peter Guzzardi, Linda Loewenthal, and Shaye Areheart for supporting and helping with the creation of this book.

Carolyn Rangel for organizing my life!

Special acknowledgment to Mike Shannon, President/CEO of KSL Recreation, and La Costa Resort and Spa, especially Ted Axe, Vice President and General Manager, Larry Kaufman, Director of Sales and Marketing, and Jeff Minton, Director of Golf, for giving full support to the programs of the Chopra Center for Well Being, including the Golf for Enlightenment Program.

And thank you to Mitchell Spearman, teacher extraordinaire.

Contents

GOLF FOR ENLIGHTENMENT

*

Foreword

BY JESPER PARNEVIK

I hate this #!&%#&!#%!!! game! I will never touch a golf club again!!

There is probably not one golfer who has never uttered these words. Still, golfers keep coming back the next day to give it another shot. Why? The answer is simple. Golf is the most brilliant game ever invented! What other game could turn seemingly intelligent and sane people into complete lunatics in a matter of seconds?

No other sport gives you the roller-coaster ride of emotions that golf does. The peaks consist of pure ecstasy and the lows are full of despair and anger. The danger lies in letting the latter get the upper hand.

I remember the year I turned pro. I was twenty-one and full of confidence. I could not wait to go out and win every tournament. To say the least, my expectations were very high. But the results didn't follow. I tried harder and harder, but played worse and worse! My frustration was beyond measure. My endless hours on the range started to seem like a complete waste of time. Every time I stepped up on the first tee, my mind was a welter of positions and swing thoughts. I decided to take a break and look for new ways to practice and improve.

I have always had an open mind and I love reading books and listening to tapes in my car. By coincidence I picked up a tape series by Deepak Chopra called *Magical Mind, Magical Body*. It had nothing to do with golf, but changed my approach to golf and life forever. Deepak mixes Eastern philosophies with Western logic in a way that is very easy to comprehend. He showed me new ways to think, eat, sleep, and practice. My biggest realization was that golf (and life) was not a game I could control, nor could I dominate it. It is a game of letting go. A golfer's biggest opponent is not the golf course or the other players. It's that little voice in your head whispering, "DON'T HIT IT IN THE WATER." When you can make that voice your best friend instead of your worst enemy, your possibilities are endless. In this book Deepak will give you all the tools and directions to do just that. I can't guarantee you will break par straight away, but you will definitely open your mind to a new world.

Golf is the most brilliant, intelligent, and fun game ever invented, and Deepak will show you that life is too! So sit back and enjoy the first golf book by one of the greatest teachers of our time.

A NEW WAY TO PLAY

✳

Golf for Enlightenment is the story of an Everyman named Adam who begins with a terrible round of golf and ends up mastering the game, an achievement he never dreamed possible. He does this through an extraordinary and mysterious teacher, a young woman named Leela. She instructs him in things that at first seem fantastic and mystical but which, in time, turn out to contain great practical wisdom.

I didn't play the game when this book was conceived. Golf was just an image caught out of the corner of my eye as I walked past airport televisions. Then one day on a long flight from Atlanta to California I was seated next to a man who was studying a golf magazine with rapt attention. Every few minutes he called on his airplane phone to Dallas, anxiously inquiring about tee times.

"You must love the game," I said casually. He turned a twisted smile toward me.

"I think I almost hate it," he replied. "I obsess about golf, and you know what? I walk off the course mad as hell. My scores don't go down. Nobody can talk to me without getting an earful of my whining. It's the worst thing I'll never let go of."

The seed of this book was planted in that moment, when a stranger blurted out his love-hate relationship to the game. If golf doesn't bring joy and satisfaction, I mused, something has been lost. Perhaps it could be brought back. The next step occurred when I met my first actual golf professional. She showed up at the Chopra Center in San Diego to be treated for a lifelong history of migraines.

"I was destined for golf from birth," my visitor told me. "Or perhaps before. I think I got my first lessons in the womb, since my mother watched so much golf on TV. It worked. I had talent, I got good. But for as long as I can remember, I've also been crippled by these agonizing headaches."

I decided to learn more about her game while focusing on curing the migraines, since the two had been connected almost from the beginning. We talked about the spiritual side of playing. Golf has always had its mysteries, but they have

✳

rarely been addressed in spiritual terms. After the visiting professional was relieved of her headaches with a course of mind–body treatments, she began to agree that golf could be approached in a new way. We formed a team. She would begin a program to teach golf as part of the Chopra Center (it became the most successful first-year offering in our history), and I would try to articulate exactly what makes golf spiritual and to explore the wisdom golf can bring to everyday life. That is the goal of this book.

Why are we here? We exist not to pursue happiness, which is fleeting, or outer accomplishment, which can always be bettered. We are here to nourish the self. The self is the source of your personal reality. All perceptions come back to the self. All emotions come back to the self. All ideas come back to the self. In golf you succeed or fail according to all three.

First, perception. Golf begins and ends with seeing the ball. Minuscule sensations streaming into your body affect where the ball will go, down to one blade of grass on the putting surface. When your perception is clear and concentrated, the ball seems to aim itself directly at the hole with the force of inevitability. Golf can't be mastered without totally clear perception.

Next, emotions. Tournaments are won on Sunday because when players of equal skill attack the course, their emotions decide the outcome. Fear and anxiety are enormously amplified in this game; the tiniest tension in a major muscle group can throw the swing off drastically. Golf can't be mastered until you confront your emotions.

Finally, ideas. Golf requires creative thinking because no two rounds are ever the same. Every new lie is a challenge, and as the player looks up from the ball to consider wind, temperature, moisture, distance to the hole, and terrain, there is much for the mind to ponder. If your thinking is rigid, the game can't be mastered.

My visiting professional, Wendy, took me on as a pupil. Because of a deep passion for cricket as a boy, I found it not too hard to learn the basics of the swing. My teacher congratulated me on having no bad habits. Some of my first shots sprayed wildly, and others landed surprisingly close to the hole. I was also astonished by the wellspring of emotions that erupted from hidden places inside me. I got frantically excited when a long putt went in; blood rose to my face if Wendy unwittingly smiled when I missed the ball completely. Any claim that "this is only a game" crumbled like a weak seawall in a hurricane.

I realized that this is one activity you cannot escape or take lightly. It holds tight, it seduces, it gives instant reward then snatches it back a moment later. In a fair world there would be a sign posted at every first tee, DO NOT FEED OR DISTURB THE GAME. IT BITES.

But the self can be your ally in taming the game. I hasten

to add that you do not need a metaphysical bent to open this book. Its seven brief, pointed lessons are meant for every golfer who has devoted long hours trying to improve his or her game. Golf is a billion-dollar industry devoted entirely to hope. The results of all this effort and expense are not always positive. The "perfect" or model swing remains ever elusive. This is because a mechanistic approach, based solely on technique, has built-in limitations. By constantly reminding yourself of the many elements in a "perfect" swing, you may gain a degree of objectivity, but you lose your self. Since the self is all-important in golf, I propose an approach that is centered there.

You Can Master this Game

In our fable, which is the first part of each chapter, Leela teaches Adam how to find himself a little more each time he returns for his lesson. "How long will it take to make me a master of the game?" he asks, not really believing she can do it at all. "We're not going to take any time," she replies. "We're going to do it now."

Now is the only time that really exists in golf. The swing is always in the present, and when you walk up the fairway to address the ball again, the present moment is once more at hand. Enlightenment is nothing more than mastering that mysterious place called now, where intention and attention come together. Leela shows Adam how to master the ever-renewing moment, and in so doing, she teaches him how to master the game of life.

One day, very early in my learning, I had an epiphany. I had been training myself to swing at the ball in a way that will seem unique. I prepare for every shot by imagining a line that runs from my heart to the ball. I push my diaphragm in and out at the navel with a few conscious breaths, an exercise used in Yoga. This special breathing is for relaxation; the line from my heart to the ball is for concentration. Finally I place my tongue against the roof of my mouth to stop the internal dialogue in my mind—again, a technique from Yoga. When I do swing, the stroke is soft, easy, and natural. The ball soars. On that particular day, I finished my round and walked off the course. For some reason, nothing changed. My mind continued to remain quiet, events flowed around me, and I looked on whatever happened with a sense of peace.

The same soft, easy, natural style that had become part of my game continued seamlessly into the rest of my day. I remembered that in the ancient scriptures of India, the highest wisdom is to see the universe from God's perspective, not as a machine, a work of art, a testing ground for karma, or a vast theater. Certainly life has all these qualities. But ultimately, the ancient sages declared, life is *leela*—a game.

Leela doesn't mean a fierce combat. The divine game isn't a competition, but play for the sheer joy of it. It has the total innocence that comes naturally to young children. In that moment my epiphany was this: *leela* is never lost. Anyone's life can be innocent, natural, easy—and it can soar. Until you reach that state, the stress of life will take its toll. Frustration and suffering are the result of innocence lost. As seen from the highest perspective, we are making a mistake to confine ecstasy to heaven and the hereafter. We have failed to accept the divine gift that makes heaven out of life on earth.

If you think I have taken a huge leap from a round of golf to some vision of utopia, then you're absolutely right. Come and make the same journey. It takes a leap of vision to master life and play it to the fullest. "When you look around, there is eternity in every direction," one spiritual teacher told his disciple. "People don't see eternity because their vision is too narrow. Yet nothing can alter it or make it go away."

Everyone's existence falls within narrow boundaries and habits, old conditioning and low expectations.... If you approach golf the wrong way, trying to manage its mechanics from the level of ego, these limitations are reinforced. If you approach golf the right way, letting your spirit be free to enjoy the *leela,* these limitations disappear.

Playing in the Garden of Eden

Golf is played in a manmade Eden, a garden. The setting is made beautiful to refresh the senses, and when you step onto the course you have a second chance at paradise.

Approaching the game from spirit, golf is no longer about winning but about growing. As much as some people make this game their religion, they haven't yet found its spiritual core. Golf is meant to be a journey to mastery, and when you achieve that mastery, your life in general will be enormously expanded, far beyond anything you now imagine.

The Garden of Eden isn't a physical place but an inner state. Golf is so addictive, I believe, because it tantalizes us with the hope of returning to a place where spirit is exalted. It's not shooting below par but above yourself that makes the game so seductive. Who would not want to return to the joy described by King Solomon in the following lines?

> *My eyes are radiant with your light,*
> *My ears delight in your music,*
> *My nostrils are filled with your fragrance.*
> *My face is covered with your dew.*
> *You have made me see all things shining,*
> *You have made me see all things new.*
> *I am bathed in celestial light, and I have become like*
> *Paradise.*

This exalted state sounds very far from practical reality. How can this really help my game? Where is the grit, the drive, the struggle? Nowhere. Mastery of golf means finding this exalted spiritual state and turning it into an everyday experience. The spiritual sages tell us that we get lost in symbols and thus forget our essence. Your score is just such a symbol. It stands for success or failure, for reaching a goal set in advance, for competing against peers and foes. Tying your self-image to your score will almost certainly taint the game and in the end destroy it as a source of pleasure. Even if that doesn't happen, the score is not a good symbol for the inner rewards of the game. Spiritual experience is not located in a zone either above or below par. Whether you call it going back to Eden or back to yourself, words are just symbols, too. The essence is taking joy in the expression of spirit, wherever it takes you.

Golf is a path, yet there are many subtle ways to stray from it. Being grim and businesslike about your game, grinding out the round when you feel you have already lost it, enforcing your private code of behavior on other players . . . this extraneous activity leads to chaos, and most players who indulge in it feel angry and frustrated round after round. I knew there was another way. Just as in life, frustration leads to bitterness, and anger destroys the capacity for joy. It's through tiny losses more than big ones that we have all forgotten the innocence of *leela*.

This book is about how to get it back.

MASTER OF THE GAME

✳

You're going to be great. Just do what I say.

It began for Adam Seaver, a golfer in the Boston metro area, on the ninth hole one Sunday afternoon. August had brought one of those dog days with heavy clouds brooding overhead. The birds were sleeping in the trees to escape the heat. Adam had just made a horrible tee shot—a low, limping hook that wound up in the rough.

He blinked in disbelief. The ball had barely made it eighty yards. But then everything had been going badly. His body was full of tension from past disasters. After he went bogey, bogey, double bogey on the sixth, seventh, and eighth holes, Adam's partners had stopped saying "It's only a game." They talked about the stock market and moved on.

Adam was so angry he didn't even set up his next shot and ended up whiffing it. Without pausing, he hacked at it again. A second whiff. This time his shoulders whirled around so fast that he almost toppled over.

Adam felt the blood rush to his face. He was sure he could hear muffled guffaws from the foursome behind. They were waiting on the tee, watching him make a fool of himself eighty yards out. His own group, feeling pellets of rain, had rushed ahead to the green.

"Stand back, take a look, give it one practice swing, then fire," Adam muttered, repeating the ritual drilled into him by the teaching professional.

His next attempt, a choppy savage swipe, cut a half-moon into the cover of the ball. It jumped up like a wounded duck and flew straight across the fairway into the opposite rough.

"Lying four," one of the spectators shouted from the tee.

Only one thing was on Adam's mind at that moment, and it wasn't this cruel endeavor they call a game: He only begged fate to get everybody's eyes off him. So he trotted across the fairway, snatched a lofted club, and stared the ball down again. It grinned up at him with its new crooked smile.

This time I'm going to kill you, he promised.

Whack!

It took a safari to find the shot, which went a long way but veered wickedly right. Adam's caddy was up for it. A new

32

✳

kid, he was getting far too much entertainment value out of this round.

"It's a terrible lie. Want me to show you?" he said helpfully, pointing into the woods.

"Not if you want to live," Adam muttered between his gritted teeth. He went in alone with a wedge, hacking at the dead brush. Spiderwebs clung to his sweating face. Something low to the ground slithered away. Now it was coming down to survival.

He got to his ball, which was half-buried in mud and slimy leaves. Gray drizzle was filtering through the pines, gathering in big cold drops that plunked on the back of Adam's neck. He was past hating the rude onlookers, the treacherous hazards, the dismal weather, his bad luck, his awful swing, and even himself. He couldn't remember feeling more alone.

That's when the voice said, "You're going to be great."

Adam stood back and peered around.

"Hello?" he called.

A stranger stepped out from the shadows of the pines. He looked somewhat older than Adam's thirty-six years. He was lean but fairly short with dark hair. His clothes hung neatly on him, defying the muggy August damp.

"You are going to be a master of the game," the stranger repeated calmly.

"What are you talking about?" The words flew out of Adam's mouth, loaded with suspicion and humiliation. "I'm getting killed here."

"And not for the first time," the stranger said, fixing his large, steady eyes on Adam. "I've been there, too, believe me." It was too dark to make out if his eyes were brown or the deepest blue.

Adam's brain wasn't taking much in. He felt confused, on top of being in hell. "Is your ball around here somewhere?" he asked impatiently.

"No."

"So it's still my shot?"

"Yes." The man turned a pale face up to the clouds. "It'll start coming down soon. No rest for the wicked."

"I guess you're trying to cheer me up. I appreciate it." Adam's voice croaked. He should have turned back to his hopeless lie, but something inside him was grateful for the interruption.

"I'm not trying to cheer you up. You're going to be great." It was the third or fourth time the stranger had said as much, but the first time that Adam really heard him. The stranger nodded faintly. "Good. But you have to do what I say."

"Why should I?" asked Adam. He stepped backward. The stranger had a presence that disturbed him, or perhaps it was his sudden appearance from nowhere. Adam could feel something squish beneath his shoe.

"You just buried your ball," the stranger remarked.

"I know." In that moment Adam wished he could sink along with it.

The stranger said, "Don't look so desperate. I think we still have a little wiggle room here."

"For the shot?" Adam said, disbelieving.

"No, for you."

At that instant the stranger's prophecy came true as the heavens opened. The downpour was perfectly timed to get Adam off the hook. Now he could head back to the club-house and forget this day ever happened. No one in his four-some would laugh at him—they all owed him from past business deals or longtime friendship. Already Adam could feel a faint twinge of hope. He'd start over next Sunday. There were still a few good shots left in his game, and with a little tweaking from the teaching professional . . .

"Stop thinking that way and listen." The stranger's voice cut sharply through the sizzling rain. Adam was startled.

"I've got to go. They're waiting," he lied.

"Take the first dirt road past the reservoir, the one accessed off the old highway. You know where," the stranger said, rais-ing his voice as if he had to reach Adam through a thick wall.

"No, I don't," Adam retorted, lying again. He could recall the old two-lane highway from his childhood in the village. No one used it anymore except for teenage couples seeking a stretch of abandoned darkness.

The stranger didn't contradict him. "Just go there," he said.

"Why?"

The man's back was already turned, and in a few seconds he had moved swiftly away. Adam emerged from the thicket looking around. His caddy, posted under an ancient oak, had the decency to open an umbrella and hold it over Adam's head without being asked.

Adam fought with himself for several days, wondering whether to go. He worried about getting into danger, but that didn't make much sense. The decisive moment, really, came when his younger brother, Ethan, asked if they could play golf together. No blood of his was going to witness Adam being humiliated. When Adam decided to go, he kept it from everyone.

The first dirt road off the old highway was easy to find. It was overgrown on both sides, a long track of waving rye grass running between old tire ruts. Adam turned his car down the road and proceeded several miles just to confirm that he was wasting his time. Old woods crept near the track and hid it from the sun every few yards. If he hadn't been paying attention, Adam would have missed the shack entirely.

He stopped, looking back at the long tail of dry summer dust kicked up by his car, and got out. This had to be it. Even the ruts ended here, as the road melted into scrub and shadows. The shack itself was made of weathered gray planking. It was larger than a tool shed but too small to hold cows or much more than a large tractor. Adam walked up to the door and noted with surprise that the hinges were new. He opened it. The darkness inside was damp, but instead of smelling like mildew, it had a faint whiff of fresh-cut fairways. It was a smell that invited him in.

When his eyes adjusted, Adam saw that his first impression had been mistaken. The shed wasn't empty, not quite. From the ceiling hung a loose net reaching to the floor, which itself was not boards or dirt but green imitation turf. Adam had seen this setup before—it was an indoor practice range. There had been one like it in the basement of his grandfather's retirement condo in Florida. The object was to hit golf balls into the net from close range, and the attached meter told you how far you had theoretically hit the shot. Adam remembered that as a boy of twelve he had whacked a ball hard enough to make the meter read 250 yards. It was one of his best memories, actually.

Adam wasn't surprised to see a few stray golf balls on the ground, and near them, propped against a cloudy window, a rusty two iron.

All right, he thought. He picked up the club and lined up a ball on the plastic turf. Taking an easy half-swing, he struck a flat arc into the net. Nothing happened, since there were no gauges to read the shot.

"You're here early." The voice behind him was that of a young woman. Adam whirled around.

"You sneak up on people," he retorted, half in surprise and half in accusation. The girl shrugged and smiled.

"You won't get much out of the machine unless you turn it on," she remarked, reaching for a switch on the wall. Adam had missed it on first inspection, and like the hinges the switch looked new. With a flick the girl turned on the overhead lights and at the same time projected an image onto the back wall. In place of a blank wooden expanse, Adam saw a green fairway. It was wide and straight with a slight elevation at the end. He could see the tip of the flagstick somewhere in the distance.

"Is that okay? I thought it was too soon for doglegs or fairway bunkers," the girl asked.

"Who are you?" Adam was still spooked. The young woman couldn't have been more than twenty at most. His question made her pause, as if she didn't expect it or needed a second to make up a plausible answer. She was slight, with bare tanned shoulders and ash-blond hair tied up under her golf cap. She was wearing a white sleeveless shirt and blue shorts. Her face was open and pleasant, the face of someone who got things done without having to set her jaw.

"I'm Leela," the girl finally said.

"Okay." Adam doubted it, despite her disarming smile.

"You knew I'd be here. Who was that man who sent you here?"

"No one you have to worry about. Want to take another shot, or should I just comment on the first one?" asked Leela.

"That wasn't a shot," Adam protested, waving his club at the old dangling net and the slide projection behind it.

"It's always a shot," Leela said. "Try again and let me see."

The authority in her voice rattled him, even though she spoke quietly. Adam stood just over six feet, and Leela barely came up to his shoulder.

Adam teed up a second ball. He felt unsteady, but Leela tucked in his right elbow with one light touch.

"Now," she said.

Without hesitation, Adam took back the club. As he swung, he felt the weight of the head moving with him, like a rock at the end of a string. He came through, the rock pulling against him at first, then joining his motion and making it stronger. There was a solid crack at contact, and the follow-through was like butter.

Wow, Adam thought. He watched the ball soar in a high, floating arc. It seemed to hang in the air a long time before easing itself back to earth about 220 yards out.

"I liked that one," Leela said. "Did you?" She walked

over and picked up the two balls from the net. Adam couldn't believe it for a second.

"I saw the ball fly. I mean, it went up, and I saw it sail until it landed," he said before his voice trailed off.

"Let me show you something," said Leela. Adam stepped back and she teed up a ball. He was still half-dazed from his own shot, so he didn't watch her closely. But when he heard the crack of the club head against the ball, his eyes riveted into focus. He saw her ball sail up and up in a much higher arc than his. For a second it seemed as if the ball floated motionless in the air, and his entire awareness was suspended with it. As if in slow motion, he saw the ball descend toward the expanse of green, which instead of being distant was suddenly below him. Without warning, time accelerated; the ball dropped and landed in the center of the hole.

Adam almost jumped out of his skin with excitement. "How did you *do* that?" he said.

"Do what?" asked Leela, looking fairly pleased.

"Didn't you see? You aced it!" Adam exclaimed. "I was right there with the ball, and it sailed right in."

For some reason a hole in one didn't seem to make Leela's day. She picked up her ball from the net and dusted it off with the tail of her shirt. "We've got to sweep this place up," she remarked to no one in particular.

"I saw your ball!" Adam almost shouted. "That's not possible."

"Okay," said Leela, not offering any further explanation.

"It's not just okay," Adam protested. Before he could blurt out anything more, Leela pointed her finger into the distance. Adam looked where she was pointing at the projection. The top of the flagstick. He squinted a little, looking closer. A faint motion. The flag was fluttering in the breeze.

Oh my God, Adam thought.

"It's the machine. They sent a good one. You should be happy," Leela said. "So, this time tomorrow?" She adjusted the visor of her cap and began to walk out. Adam reached for her arm but missed.

"What are you doing?" he asked, not daring to believe any of this.

"I'm going to make you great," Leela said. With the same cool authority, she reached for the door and opened it. A shaft of August light struck Adam's eyes, turning Leela into a black silhouette for a fraction of a second. The next moment, Adam was alone in the dark shed. He hadn't seen her flick off the switch.

Adam knew he would be back.

LESSON 1

✳

Be of One Mind

The next day, Wednesday, Adam left work early. If he put in an hour at the shack, he could still make it home before dinner. He had packed some golf shoes in the trunk along with his clubs. Excitement had started to build in him right after lunch, and between four and four-thirty the hands of the clock seemed to be glued in place.

Now he was driving up the old dirt track hearing the swish of the tall rye grass brush the bottom of his car.

What if she's not there? Adam thought. *What if last Sunday was some kind of strange fluke?* Leela hadn't even set a time for today, so how could she possibly expect to meet him?

She'll be there. Adam didn't have to think the words.

He stopped at the shack. It looked as empty as before, but

when he opened the door, carrying his clubs over his shoulder and his shoes in one hand, Leela was sweeping the floor, humming softly to herself.

She greeted Adam over her shoulder as she emptied her dustpan out one of the broken windows.

"Where's your car?" Adam asked.

"Let's see you putt," Leela replied.

Adam stood there a moment wondering why Leela avoided his questions. He decided that this wasn't the moment to challenge her. "If we're putting, I guess I won't be needing these," he mumbled, holding out his black golf shoes.

"You'll need everything you usually wear. Do you have a cap?" asked Leela. She put away her broom, went over to the wall, and flicked the switch. The lights came on as before, but this time the image projected on the wall was of a large, flat putting green.

"Yeah, I have it," said Adam, pulling a rolled-up cap from his back pocket. "I really need to wear this?"

Leela nodded, her face serious. "We're starting with the fundamentals today. Details count if you're going to have a perfect game."

Adam looked up from tying his shoes. "Perfect?" He grinned doubtfully. "How long do you think that's going to take? I'd have to come back here for ten years. I'd have to come back with a new body, too."

"It's not going to take time," said Leela. "You're going to do it now."

Adam would have laughed raucously except that his body had started trembling in a peculiar ripple, as if energy was rolling from his head to his toes and at the same time outward from the center of his chest to his fingertips. *What was that?* he thought, but the sensation faded before he could panic. In that split second, something inside him shifted ever so slightly.

"Be of one mind," Leela said. Her voice was quiet, but it filled Adam's mind.

"Be of one mind?" he said, turning it into a question. Leela nodded.

"Now, let's see you putt," she said. Moving quickly, she dropped a ball on the green plastic turf, then she flicked her eyes toward the putting green. Adam took his stance and a few practice putting strokes, the way he'd been taught.

"Be of one mind," he muttered to himself.

"You don't need to repeat it," said Leela.

"I thought it was a mantra or something," said Adam.

"No."

Then what's the point? Adam grumbled, but he kept the thought to himself. He took a few more practice strokes. "Is my grip okay?" he asked.

"Just look at the ball," said Leela.

Adam glanced at the ball, then at the image on the back

wall. It looked like an ordinary slide projection, nothing magical like that first day. Adam wondered where he was supposed to aim. He envisioned an imaginary line running along the plastic turf and up the wall to the hole. *Here goes nothing,* he thought.

"No, wait," Leela interrupted. "Look at the ball."

"I am," Adam said, keeping his head down for the putt.

"You aren't," Leela insisted. She walked over and took the putter from his hands. "This might help. Hold your hands in place without the club. Now look at the ball."

Adam followed her instructions, but at first he was embarrassed—it reminded him of playing air guitar in his college drinking days. But then there was another ripple of energy in his body, this time fainter than the first. The atmosphere grew quiet; he became aware that his mind was subsiding, draining like a basin as his thoughts swirled down and away.

Look at the ball.

This time there were no words—the ball grabbed his whole attention. He couldn't help but look at it as it zoomed in larger and larger until it filled his vision.

"Okay, that's about right," said Leela. "Don't look at me. Just take the club."

Adam felt the putter sliding back into his hands. He took a second to adjust his grip, then glanced at the cup. It was no longer just a hole projected on the wall. It was right in front of him. The surface under his feet was grass, and he saw a perfect true line between himself and the cup. His heart began to pound. Fighting his excitement, Adam drew back the club.

"Not yet," said Leela. "Look at the hole."

Without protest, he knew what she meant. He had to see the hole the way he saw the ball. Adam relaxed. He was growing more familiar with what it took. He waited, then his mind cleared again, accompanied by that faint energy wave in his body. The hole grew larger and larger, just as the ball had, until it was as wide as a basketball hoop.

"Now?" he whispered. The anticipation of sinking this one beautiful, perfect putt was almost too much for him.

With a click, Leela turned off the lights, and the image of the green vanished. Adam stood up with a jerk. "Why did you do that? What about my putt?" he yelled. His voice was harsh enough to surprise him.

"The putt went in," said Leela.

"I didn't even hit it. How could it go in?"

"Because it had to. Putts that go in *have* to. You saw the ball, you saw the hole. Nothing else goes into the equation. Congratulations."

Adam flung his putter to the floor. The doubt and confusion that he had been suppressing since he met the man in the woods now welled up. "Thanks for the mind game, but I quit. I don't know who you are or who that guy was who sneaked up on me last Sunday or what you want from me.

But I do know this: I'm out of here." He felt furious and helpless at the same time.

"This was a good lesson," said Leela calmly.

"Right." Adam braced himself for another blast of uncontrollable rage, but it didn't come.

Leela said, "No, really. We're going deep, and this is good." In fact, she did look very pleased. Leela had one of those faces that didn't hide what she was feeling.

Adam's torn breathing began to find a rhythm again. He was still just as confused, but something big had broken loose. He felt drained. It took another moment before he could talk coherently.

"What was that?" he asked.

Leela said, "You always have to expect a little discharge of energy. It's like smoke or after burn. Don't worry."

"Exploding like that is normal?" asked Adam. His arms and legs felt as weak as a kitten's.

"It depends on how much you've been holding in. In your case, a lot," said Leela.

"And now I'm holding less?"

"Yes. It was a good lesson," Leela repeated. "And your putt did go in. Trust me."

Playing the Game

The first lesson is about perception. There are moments, as every player knows, when the ball seems to change size.

There are moments when the hole does the same thing, or when a distant green suddenly jumps so near and you feel you could reach out and touch the flagstick. These are not optical illusions but a key to the game. A longtime player on the PGA tour, Billy Mayfair, set the scoring record for nine holes. He did this by making eight consecutive birdies (itself a record) followed by a par. His total score for the back nine was nine under par. When asked what happened during his round, Mayfair said, "Every hole looked as big as a bathtub. All I did was try to get out of my own way." In moments of altered perception, anything is possible.

Perception is what your mind makes of the data streaming into it from everywhere. In golf, a player's perceptions are particularly complex. Nature surrounds you, capricious and unpredictable. There are light and wind to consider, temperature and distance, the undulation of terrain, along with obstructing trees and tall rough. All must enter the equation of your shot. At every moment these factors shift. The wind whips and whirls. You can be faced with an uphill, downhill, or sidehill lie. A putt may begin in sunlight and end in dappled shade.

If you get distracted by the shifting picture, your swing will suffer. Most players are in a state of distraction even when they think they are not. When there are no distractions, whatever you look at becomes all-important. The surrounding scenery loses its grip on your mind. The sages of India call this "one-pointed attention," the ability to see one thing and one thing only.

In golf, your perception must remain on the ball. Over and over again, teaching professionals will say, "Keep your eye on the ball." But few players can do that consistently. By its very nature, perception tends to wander. It is trained to scan its surroundings. Pleasure comes from casting a wide net and bringing back as many charming sensations as possible. (A roving eye has doomed more golf games than it has marriages.)

The mystery of perception is how it can be wide open and one-pointed at the same time. You have to keep your eye on the ball, but you mustn't be hypnotized by it. Your senses need to remain aware of all those outside factors—the lie of the ball, the terrain, wind, temperature, and so on—or you won't be able to adjust your swing to fit the situation. These two demands, being wide open and being totally focused, are opposites.

The mind creates opposites. Spirit reconciles them.

Most players, once they realize how important it is to see the ball, fight against all the distractions that want to pour in. They struggle to keep outside noises from their mind, for example, and try not to swing until everything is as quiet as possible. But you can never completely control the environment, and even if you succeeded, there is the inner environment with its constant chatter. The struggle to be one-pointed leads to an inner war. War breeds tension, and being tense will ruin every shot.

What if you decided not to go to war with yourself? Concentration comes naturally when your desire to see is unblocked. When you are in love, for example, you cannot take your eyes off your beloved. There's no inner war, no opposing urge to let your attention wander. In some way you need to love the ball just as much.

You will love the ball only when you are of one mind.

The first lesson is really the last lesson and all the ones in between. Getting out of your own way means that instead of seeing yourself in separation, you see yourself in union. At that moment you will see the ball, love the ball, and be at one with it. All three happen at once. The desired shift in perception—that magical enhancement that makes the ball zoom in size and widens the hole into a bathtub—is the result of being one with the ball, not the cause. You can't force the ball to grow, but you can nourish the cause.

We know that close attention nourishes a child, while inattention and neglect leads to very poor results. Nourishment is just a relationship based on the heart. Nourishing the ball means making it as alive as you are. It becomes fluid, cooperative, willing. Your relationship becomes one of trust. You aren't out there to whack the ball or punish it, to take out your frustrations or vent your rage. Players who relate to the ball in those ways are abusing it, which comes back to them as bad shots. (You may smile at the idea of loving the ball, but just watch how many abused balls get their revenge in the end!) When I am out with a teaching professional, I follow my instructions to the letter as best I can, but there's an inner dimension that is also at work. Before I hit my drive from the tee, I nourish my relationship to the ball by saying, "You're part of me. Right now, I am still and you are still. When I move, you will move. When you soar, I will soar with you."

In many traditions, this nourishment is part of what is known as mindfulness. When attention is still, calm, and focused, it is mindful. When attention is restless, wandering, and dispersed, it is unmindful. One or the other is always at work. (If you want to picture the state of mindfulness, watch Tiger Woods when he is playing at his height. His gaze is soft yet laserlike in its focus, one-pointed but deeply calm. Other great professionals demonstrate the same look. There is no more beautiful gaze in all of sport.)

In golf, the sweet spot is the small area on the face of the club that denotes perfect contact with the ball. When you hit it, you know that the mechanics of your swing have come together flawlessly. There is a satisfying solid thwack that any experienced player can hear and instantly know that the ball has been beautifully struck even before it lofts into the air on its flight.

At any given moment, you are capable of finding the sweet spot in yourself.

The sweet spot in yourself is a place that knows what to do. It is calm, unattached, at peace. From it flows any action you desire, any intention you want to accomplish. Mindfulness brings the player into his own sweet spot first, before considering the one outside him. So far as the actual face of the club goes, manufacturers of equipment brought more new players into the game when they enlarged the sweet spot, and many golfers still put a huge reliance on it. But to consistently hit the ball on the sweet spot is next to impossible for amateurs, and even top professionals have their lapses.

The secret is to make it a mental feat. See the sweet spot as a goal you will always reach because you are connected to it. I imagine an invisible string that connects my heart to the ball. When I do that, I am no longer swinging with a long stick that can waver far off course. The sweet spot and the ball are destined for each other. They belong together.

The reason this technique works is because of the sweet spot inside, a free, open zone within yourself that knows with certainty that everything will go perfectly. You go there to coordinate mind, body, and spirit. But how can you find this path every time?

I use memories but I do not allow memories to use me.

My body is just the place that my memories call home for the time being.

Stopping, calming, resting, and playing are the key.

The Vietnamese monk Thich Nhat Hanh has described four aspects that are common to Buddhist meditation: stopping, calming, resting, and healing. When these four elements come together, the result is total focus, even in the midst of enormous activity. In terms of golf, where focus is required all the time, the four steps are:

Stopping the random activity of the mind that surfaces in a constant inner dialogue with yourself.

Calming your emotions, which fuel the inner dialogue with fears, doubts, and remembered feelings from the past.

Resting your attention so that it comes to reside at a point of clear focus.

Playing the shot from stillness.

A mind that has found its natural ability to stop, be calm, and come to rest is a mind ready for action. Repeat these steps every time you address the ball, until they become second nature. If you notice that you have skipped a step, go back to it.

Learning to stop, calm, rest, and play extends far outside the game. Mindfulness is required in the game of life. It is the clear ground from which you can make decisions that can be trusted. If you find yourself in conflict, mindfulness won't always come to your aid, not immediately. But nothing else works better, and the time you spend finding your sweet spot will be abundantly repaid.

Stop the struggle, calm the emotions, rest in yourself, enjoy the play. This is the goal. At the same time, this is the means to get there.

There is always a built-in conflict between silence and activity. Silence belongs to your innermost being; activity belongs to the outer world. They are totally opposed, and even though spirit never goes to war, resolving this opposition takes a warrior's energy and attention. The battle is against those tendencies that constantly pull us away from our source. The end of the war comes when you find peace through one-pointed focus.

Applied to Life

If you can be of one mind, you can be one with anything. The trick is to close the gap of perception. Today, tell yourself that you will see something familiar with new eyes. The result can be startling, even though the techniques to accomplish this shift are simple:

Take any object that you once loved but have stopped seeing—a picture on the wall, a favorite shirt, a knickknack on your desk. Now, instead of looking at it, give it life. Make up a name and start a dialogue as if the object were alive and sharing its history with you. "I remember when we met," you might start. "It was the week before Christmas. I'd given up on finding anything nice to give X, and then I saw you. I loved the sight of you so much that I didn't give you away. I had to keep you for myself." Now, make up a response from the object. "I knew you liked me. It was obvious."

This isn't a childish game. The more imaginative and alive your dialogue, the more your attention will flow to the object. By doing so, you close the gap of perception. The same thing happens with strangers. From afar, they strike us indifferently or with irritation. Yet when you move past your aloofness and begin to talk, that warm body pressed too close to you in an airline seat becomes human, and the attention you exchange with every word causes a shift in how you perceive each other.

If you truly pay attention, there is no other. The world becomes intimate to you when you risk complete intimacy, which means a free flow of attention without holding back, setting aside beliefs, assumptions, prejudice, and expectations. To move from separateness to unity—a state of merging at once delicate and incredibly powerful—doesn't happen all at once. Yet there is no secret to achieving this state of communion. All it takes is the willingness to allow the flow of attention. If you begin to look upon everything as alive, it will come closer and want to be known. In the simple act of seeing yourself in the other, enlightenment becomes possible.

LESSON 2

✴

Let the Swing Happen

Adam spent the next few days feeling strange. Leela hadn't told him he couldn't play a round of golf, but Adam didn't want to. His experiences in the shack would never be repeated on a real course. Or maybe they would. Maybe Leela could make that happen, too. It wasn't as if Adam could guess the limits of her abilities. She was the magical girl with the magic machine. Beyond those two facts, his brain whirred helplessly. Perhaps like the images on the wall, Leela was really a projection. Or an angel.

Dreaming and speculation filled his head for the next few days, until one evening, as he drove home from work, Adam started to pass a truck. At that instant he heard a shrill honk as a sports car leaped out of his blind spot. The driver, who had been accelerating just as Adam pulled out, looked as alarmed as Adam felt—his eyes dilated, his skin pale and sweaty. Two seconds later, it was over. Adam had swerved back quickly, and the sports car gunned past both him and the truck.

As the spurt of adrenaline faded, Adam had a thought. You can't see someone's dilated eyes in a side-view mirror. But he had. For an instant the other driver's face had been right there in front of him. Shaken, Adam pulled off the road at the next gas station. As he stepped out, he heard a roaring sound like the cascade of water through a storm drain. He looked behind him. It was the gas being pumped by another driver across the island. When the same man pulled a quarter out of his pocket to go buy a cola, Adam was sure he could read the date on the coin: 1987.

"Mister," he said.

"What?" The man turned around.

Adam couldn't bring himself to ask to check the coin. "Ah, nothing." The man nodded curtly and left. Adam got back in the car and drove away, touched by a sudden feeling of awe. What had Leela brought about?

Saturday morning came, and Adam awoke knowing it was time to return. Whatever sudden urge made him throw his clubs into the car and drive at breakneck speed out to the old highway, it was an instinct he had to trust. A strong wind kicked up a dusty plume behind his car. The wind seemed to grow as he approached the shack, and when he stopped, Adam stepped out into a furious dust cloud that hid everything from view.

It won't be there, he feared. Then he heard an open door banging in the wind. Adam had to crouch to fight his way to the shack. He stumbled in and reached to pull the door shut behind him.

"Don't," a voice said. The shack was murky with dust, and though he couldn't make her out, Adam knew it must be Leela.

"Why not?" Adam asked, starting to cough in the choking brown haze.

"We need it. Hold on." Adam could barely make her out as Leela briskly opened all the windows in the shack. After a moment the dust cleared, but the wind blew harder than ever. It blew straight through the building as if its walls didn't exist. Leela flicked the switch. Before him Adam saw a long fairway, but not the one from the first day. This one looked like a course in England or Scotland. The grass was choppy and straw yellow instead of green. The terrain rolled like a pasture, except that no pasture ever had so many potholes and bunkers scattered everywhere.

"Cows would break their legs," Adam muttered.

"Really," Leela agreed. She seemed to enjoy the jest. "They have a lot of weather here, too," she said. In fact the fairway, as Adam looked closer, ended in a clump of scraggly old trees whose leaves were blowing with the same wind that howled through the shack.

"Bring them closer if you like," said Leela. "Take in as much as you can. Give yourself maximum information before you swing."

Even before she'd finished, Adam's sight was roving over the course. Like the day when he had flown with Leela's ball to the pin, he found himself able to swoop over the bunkers, following the curving line of thick gorse on the left and the rail of poplars that lined a railroad track on the right. It was a wonderful sensation, but not one of flying, because Adam hadn't left the spot he was standing on; his eyes simply summoned whatever he wanted to see—details zoomed in and out, getting bigger and smaller at will.

"Am I really doing this?" Adam asked. He had enough presence of mind this time not to be dumbfounded.

"You tell me," said Leela. "Have you been practicing? Seeing the ball, I mean."

Adam felt self-conscious. "No, I didn't think I'd be able to without you, without being here. But there was this one incident—"

"Good, so now you can remember to practice," Leela said, cutting him off by handing him a three wood. "Let's play this hole. You have the honor."

Adam wondered if she was kidding, since the honor goes to the player with the best score on the last hole. But he did as she told him, teeing up his ball on the plastic turf. Leela had taken down the net, giving him a clear view of the fairway.

"I tend to slice it," Adam mumbled, eyeing the dense, thorny gorse bushes on the left. At that moment the wind shrieked so loudly that his words flew away. His ball toppled off the tee, and Adam dropped to a squat, holding on to his club to keep it from being blown out of his hands. "What are we doing here?" he shouted.

"Enjoying the game," Leela shouted back. She replaced his ball on the tee, but it blew off again immediately.

"It's going to keep doing that, you know," Adam pointed out.

"Then you'd better hit it fast," said Leela. Apparently she was serious. Adam took his stance—if you could call his leaning totter a stance—and when Leela teed him up again, he took a blind swipe with the wind flat in his face. Amazingly, he made contact. The ball, although badly topped, limped fifty feet ahead of them down the middle of the fairway.

"Let's go," Leela shouted, putting her face inches from Adam's ear. He couldn't believe she wanted him to go out there, but already Leela had slung his bag over her shoulder and was heading toward the projection.

This is going to be good, Adam thought, determined not to blink so that he wouldn't miss the exact instant when Leela melted into the image or hit the wall. But he must have blinked, because all at once they were both on the links, bending nearly double against the wind, which Adam could now see was blowing in from the rough gray seas directly behind them.

Adam felt exhilarated. Catching up with Leela as she neared his ball, he shouted, "What do you call this thing, this machine?" He waved his arms all around to indicate the vast expanse of sky and sea and turf. Every nerve in his body tingled and thrilled.

"A vision simulator," Leela shouted back. "There goes your ball. You better catch it."

Having landed in a downhill lie, Adam's ball had waited for them but was now slowly moving down the slope. "You don't expect me to run after it?" Adam asked, his voice getting husky from having to yell.

"Unless you want it to gain on you," said Leela.

Caught up in the spirit of the thing, Adam grabbed a five iron and trotted after his ball. It kept gaining momentum. "Don't I have to wait until it stops?" he yelled over his shoulder.

"Just hit it!" Leela shouted with her hands cupped over her mouth.

At that moment the ball came to rest. Adam addressed it quickly and looked up. The green was nowhere in sight, thanks to a sharp dogleg to the left. A professional would try to aim over the gorse to clear the dogleg, but Adam knew he couldn't make it. So he decided to lay up and aimed straight down the middle of the fairway. So as not to top the ball again, he dug deep. A huge divot flew up like a frightened grouse, and the ball sailed forty yards into the wind.

Adam gazed down at the hole he'd chewed out with his club. "Go on after it," Leela said. "I'll replace the divot. Unless you want to stay and dig for treasure."

Adam threw her a grin and loped off after his ball. It took another two sloppy shots to make the putting surface. The green had a hard slope and a few wrinkles like rumpled bed-clothes, but after two putts he was in. A double, if anyone was counting. Adam certainly wasn't. He picked his ball out of the hole and asked, "Where's the next hole?"

"Here," Leela said.

Adam looked around. They were back on the same tee where they'd started. "Play it again?" he asked. "Why? The wind's worse, and I'm not learning anything."

"That's because I haven't taught you anything yet. Please hit," said Leela.

They went around again. Adam's mood began to sour. He couldn't quite remember when the freezing needles of rain started to fall. *Fall* wasn't the right word, since the gale aimed them horizontally into his face and thin shirt. Silent this time, Adam played better, making it to the green in three and two putting. "Bogey," he said with just a hint of triumph, although he didn't like what was coming next.

"Your honor," said Leela cheerfully. As Adam had guessed, they were back on the original tee with the raging sea behind them, not that he could spy it anymore through the sweeping curtains of rain. Grimly he swung, barely bothering to look at the ball. It flew in a wobbly arc toward the railroad tracks. They spent five minutes searching for it under the dripping poplars, and then Adam barely had a shot to the fairway without advancing the ball. On the green in six, via a nasty deep pothole, and two putts. Quadruple bogey. Adam didn't take the ball out of the hole.

"When are you going to teach me something?" he grumbled. His whole body was chilled and exhausted; he could barely see or think. And he was too wet to bother even wringing out the sloshing cuffs of his pants.

"Soon," Leela promised.

Soon meant another couple of go-rounds. On the point of screaming, Adam refused to even open his eyes when they were once more back on the cursed tee. His hands hung like dead weights on the end of rubber bands stretched to the point of agony. His feet were cold clods without any feeling at all.

"Now," Leela said. Adam opened his eyes to see the fairway he dreaded, only all of a sudden the air was dead calm. The sun had come out, warming everything. Adam postponed his decision to lie down and die. "Now the lesson?" he asked hopefully.

Leela nodded, teeing up a fresh ball.

He sighed and addressed the ball, his grip weak and the muscles in his forearms twitching with fatigue.

"Make it a good one," Leela encouraged.

No chance of that. What Adam produced was barely a swing. He took the club all the way back and let it drop like a stone, the weight of the club head carrying it around faster than any strength he could impart. With dazed eyes, he watched the ball rise. And rise. And rise. It sailed clean and clear beyond the potholes and landed dead center in the fairway just where the dogleg turned. His mind went blank.

"Okay," said Leela. "Let's get you into some dry clothes."

Adam turned to her with amazement. "How did I do that?"

"You didn't do it. You *allowed* it," Leela said. She turned and walked away from the tee.

"That's the lesson?" he asked. "I should exhaust myself before the first hole? Maybe I could hit the ball better, but I wouldn't have enough legs to walk after it."

"No, getting you exhausted was like getting the crowd to quiet down before the shot. Your mind was talking all the time. You were giving in to frustration. Your ego wanted to whale at the ball, mostly to impress me, and your nerves kept doubting that you could even hit it. The crowd was really restless today; it got in the way all the time."

Adam had to admit that was a pretty good description of how he'd played. "But what about the wind? I didn't create that obstacle."

"You didn't?" asked Leela. Her eyes shot him a look.

"What you're telling me," Adam said, "is that I can't make a good shot until I get everything out of the way?"

"Right."

"Then teach me how to do that. Without the exhaustion, I mean," said Adam.

"Okay. When?" asked Leela.

"Now, right now," insisted Adam, who despite everything was feeling a sudden surge of strength and confidence.

Leela smiled. "Fine," she said. "When you come back."

"But next week isn't now," Adam complained, crestfallen.

"It will be," said Leela, "once we get there. You coming?"

Adam decided he'd better. Since only Leela could get them into the vision simulator, presumably only Leela could get them out.

Playing the Game

The second lesson is about getting out of your own way. Golf is an inner game with inner obstacles. Those who know this have a saying: Golf comes down to what your ego wants you to do, what your mind tells you to do, and what your nerves will let you do.

Say that you've landed in a bunker when everyone else has hit the green. They stand patiently watching while you climb down and take your stance.

Your ego tells you, "I want to blast this one into the hole. I'll show them all."

Your mind tells you, "Get this right. Stand back in your stance, hold the club firmly, get under the ball but not too much. I think that's what the pro said, isn't it?"

Your nerves tell you, "I'm about to make a fool of myself. What if I leave this ball in the bunker? Come on, everyone's watching. Just go! Now!"

When you finally swing, your ball flies blindly, in perfect accord with the mixed signals you've been sending to your body. To truly get out of your own way, you must master non-doing. This term, which is found throughout the ancient Eastern wisdom traditions, means much more than being passive. Non-doing happens when you put your trust in a higher intelligence than your individual mind, a higher will than your individual will, and a higher power than your individual power.

The mystery of non-doing is that it can accomplish far more than doing. We see this on the golf course when someone plays marvelous golf with minimal instruction. Golfers will often lament that they putted much better at the age of twelve than they do now as adults. Doubt had not yet produced its corrosive effect on a player's self-confidence. Or to put it concisely, it was easier then to get out of your own way. (The day I wrote this last sentence, I picked up a golf magazine and noticed an item about a fourteen-year-old boy in the Midwest who shot 14 under par, one stroke off the course record. A few weeks later a three-year-old had a hole in one on a par 3 course outside Chicago, hitting the ball 45 yards to break the hole-in-one record set previously by a five-year-old.)

Non-doing is innocence regained.

If the Garden of Eden could be described in one word, it would be *innocence*. Man did not have to toil there; it was a state in which struggle and effort were not needed. When you fight against your swing and struggle to keep your nerves in check, you are far from innocence. Analysts have examined and measured old movies of Bobby Jones's swing, and they've determined that its speed was only 3 percent faster than gravity. In a world where the average golfer muscles the ball on every shot, this is an amazing fact. It means that allowing the club to fall naturally from its top position in the backswing would accomplish 97 percent of what the greatest player could accomplish. I've seen this confirmed by a demonstration of one-armed swinging: A professional simply held a driver in the right hand, lifted it back, and allowed it to follow through using nothing but gravity. With good contact, the ball consistently flew about 200 yards.

Of course, a great golfer adds finesse and intelligence to

the swing, and there are times when added power is needed. In long-distance driving, the club head achieves a speed in excess of 110 miles per hour, which is far more than gravity can provide. The point is that each of us is endowed with a natural swing. Through non-doing, you let go of all the bad habits you've added to the simple motion of a club head falling to earth of its own accord.

Here are some examples of non-doing compared to its opposite, which we'll call "efforting":

Efforting muscles the swing. When the ball gets out of control, less power is required to regain that control. Non-doing builds power gradually, starting with a gravity-driven swing as the foundation.

Efforting requires constantly monitoring the body, trying to correct its inevitable mistakes. Non-doing assumes that your body is wise enough to carry through with what you tell it to do.

Efforting controls the swing. Non-doing allows the swing to happen.

Because we've all been raised to believe in the value of struggle and effort, non-doing doesn't come naturally. I discovered this myself during a recent round. Despite being in a good mood and looking forward to the game, I played horribly on the first five holes. For some reason I had lost the ability to make clean contact, so sometimes I'd be topping the ball; other times, I'd be hitting it fat, throwing up big, ugly divots. On all three levels, ego, mind, and emotion, I had lost balance. My ego was fighting to regain control and determined to hack a good game out of a bad one. My mind kept racing to remember the lost elements of my once-proud swing. My emotions steadily sank into doubt and self-criticism. (Ironically, I had been hitting the ball beautifully on the practice tee just moments before. Perhaps the seed of my downfall was overconfidence.)

Then, miraculously, as I stepped onto the sixth tee, a short par 3, I hit an amazing shot. It flew in a picture-perfect arc to the green and landed about 2 feet from the pin. As I felt my courage seep back, my playing companion made a simple, astute remark.

"I notice you play better when you're tired," he said.

He was right. Like Adam, I had taken the tough route to non-doing—I had fought as hard as I could until I had no strength left. At that point, once the struggle had run its course, the wisdom of the body took over, and the swing just happened.

Non-doing also comes naturally to us when we feel centered. Effort is directed outward, as we saw when I fought to regain my swing, but in reality the struggle is always internal—you exert effort whenever your center is lost. By *center* I mean the sweet spot inside. To find your center without effort, take the following steps:

Know that you have a center.

Know that you belong there.

Know that the path to the center takes no effort.

Each of these sentences begins with the word *know* because non-doing is just a way of remembering who you really are. You are not the struggle, and you never have been. You are the knower. In the Bhagavad Gita, the ancient Vedic text, Lord Krishna speaks of the "inward dweller" who constantly observes, touched by nothing yet part of everything. Salvation is possible on the golf course thanks to the inward dweller. He or she is the most human aspect of you, the source of all love, truth, and beauty.

And best of all, the inward dweller knows how to play golf. When you get out of the way, your natural swing reappears. It might not be as powerful as you want, but you can build on that. It is far easier to add distance to a 150-yard drive that goes straight than to pull back a 275-yard drive that betrays you. Pulling back involves finding all the myriad hidden errors and trying to correct them. This can be nearly impossible, buried as they usually are in a maze of thought, feeling, and ego. That's why big hitters who attempt to pull back to a shorter distance continue to hook and slice anyway. The problem wasn't too much power, it was the inability to be centered.

If you want to feel what it's like to be centered, just remember what it was like to play as a child. True play is effortless, joyous, alive—it is non-doing in action. The following steps will lead you there:

Once in a while, play the game without keeping score.

When you get caught up in the emotional roller coaster of play, you get pulled away from your center. Keeping score reinforces these mood swings. At the level of ego you keep hoping that your bad shots will be replaced by a string of beautiful ones. This isn't the road to mastery. No matter how many good shots you string together, you are never guaranteed you won't plunge to the depths with the next disastrous hook or the next 2-foot putt that rims the hole without going in. What you want is to become acquainted with that part of yourself that is beyond reaction, that is calm, centered, knowing, skillful, and always in control. Your ego has never delivered these qualities to you, so why not stop asking it to? Forget the score and concentrate on finding your sweet spot inside.

Forget where the ball goes.

The flight of the ball is the result of all the events preceding it, both physical and mental. Bad shots are preceded by very different events than good ones. Instead of looking at the result, start looking at the cause. Are you centered or not? A good shot is preceded by bringing together all the right ingredients—proper state of mind, precise awareness of the body, the free flow of information to your muscles, the absence of distracting and extraneous thoughts. It takes the knower within to bring you into such a state of harmony that nothing can go wrong. So while you are making the knower's acquaintance, stop trying to get your mind to do a job it can't do. Just make your preparation, align the shot, and let the ball fall where it wants to. Nothing more.

Enjoy your swing.

This is much the same as forgetting where the ball goes. When you stop keeping score, you take the element of competition out of the game, and hopefully you stop judging yourself as a good or bad player. Judgment creeps back in, however, through thoughts like "That was a terrible shot, what's wrong with you?" or "You hit that shot perfectly last week, now look what you've done." When you are centered, you won't be judgmental. The knower, being a master of the game, enjoys every swing, so you might as well start doing the same. Hit the ball in whatever way feels best, without anxiety over mechanics.

You aren't going to lose everything you were taught by devoting a few holes or a few rounds to letting go and simply enjoying your swing. If you were taught well, you already know two things: The mechanics are simple when you stop trying; the mechanics will get stored in body memory once they are practiced enough times.

Bring your energy inward and do not allow it to be wasted.

Once you have sloughed off the distractions of the score, the mechanics of your swing, and where the ball goes, you can finally approach the main task, which is learning to use your energy in a totally different way. When your energy is directed outward, it is disorganized, it ebbs and flows, it is subject to being dissipated and lost without your knowledge. Energy is meant to be fresh, strong, coherent, and channeled with great precision.

In golf, the expenditure of energy is nearly instantaneous: It starts with an intention in the brain and two seconds later ends up with terrific force smashing into the ball. At the very beginning of the energy path, you decide where the whole shot is coming from. If your ego says, "This is the shot that's going to impress everyone," or if your mind says, "This is the shot that will prove I know what I'm doing," or if your emotions say, "This is the shot that's going to make me feel great," the shot is lost before you've drawn the club head back an inch. You are working in a projection. Energy is directed to a specific outcome, and results are only an illusion before they actually happen.

There is great benefit to finding your silent core instead. Silence is the sign that you have drawn your focus back to the point of greatest power, like drawing back a bow before shooting the arrow. This is where you will meet the inward dweller. The first swing you make from your center begins the relationship that will allow life to happen.

Applied to Life

The next time you have a challenge to meet, approach it with an attitude of non-doing. The technique is not as mystical as it sounds.

First, promise yourself you will not struggle.
Second, do the minimum first, then stand back.
Third, allow answers to come from your center.

If you approach a difficult problem without struggle, a complex process will begin to unfold. Ego, emotions, and nerves will try to undo you. Not just golf but everything you do is caught between what your ego wants you to do, what your mind tells you to do, and what your nerves will let you do. These powerful forces, made stronger by years of holding sway, will inevitably try to take over. But you have to resist the urge to resist them. That part is tricky and requires patience. Yet it is all-important if you are to access an intelligence higher than your own.

The second step helps. Most of us charge from one phase of a problem to the next. So do the minimum instead. Stand back and appreciate the problem anew. Ask yourself if you see an outcome that feels satisfying, which is like a painter deciding whether his first brush stroke fits the final picture he has in mind. If you feel even slightly less than satisfied, go home for the day rather than starting over. Solutions incubate at a deep level; the subtle reaches of your self don't run forward with the speed demanded by the mind. No matter. What comes deep comes true. If your first step happens to satisfy you, you should still go home for the day. A fresh perspective could still be waiting to be born.

Finally, realize that the third step is your true goal. It isn't outward success that ever matters but whether you succeed in living from your center. Non-doing isn't superior to doing except in this one regard—it gets you used to seeing everything from your core of truth. However much you have to retrain yourself, this one goal is worth the highest price anyone could pay.

LESSON 3

✳

Find the Now and You'll Find the Shot

Adam was so wrung out from his lesson that he collapsed into bed the minute he got home. He had no memory of pulling his golf shoes off. He woke up on top of the covers blinded by white light. He must have slept from sundown straight through to dawn. When he woke up, however, he felt full of anticipation. He kept thinking about his next lesson, when Leela was going to show him the secret of the perfect swing.

Adam went through the week feeling light and loose. It seemed as if he'd lost some weight, and his shoulders dropped three inches overnight. Until that happened, Adam had never realized that he had been hunched up. What was he bracing against? Whatever it was, apparently it had gone away.

Adam noticed other changes. He stopped muttering to himself in bad traffic; he didn't drift off in meetings; the insufferably boring people at work didn't seem so tedious. Anticipation didn't account for all of this. There was something else. Then he figured it out: He wasn't pushing back. The traffic could be bad, the bores could be boring, and he could just let it all happen. His hunched shoulders had been resisting everything he had hated and everything he hadn't wanted to accept. Reality had flooded in on him, and only part of it was anything he wanted or could control. The rest threatened to drown him or run him over like a tractor trailer.

Adam was poised with a greasy hamburger halfway to his mouth when he saw all this in a flash, and he burst out laughing. What had he been thinking? You can't treat reality like a salesman at the door and say, "Just a minute, I won't let you in until I've made sure I feel okay about you." But that was exactly what he had been doing.

I've refused to let life happen.

At that moment it seemed ludicrous that he or anyone else could be so deluded as to think that they could hold life back, but in the next instant Adam felt something in his chest open. With a surge of relief he knew that he had just given himself permission to stop resisting. The greasy hamburger tasted like ambrosia.

On Thursday and Friday, as the weekend approached, he still felt exhilarated, and when he got into the car on Saturday morning, the trip to the shack took no time at all. He bounded in to see Leela waiting with a bag of clubs spread out on the floor.

"What are you doing?" Adam asked, hoping she would ask him why he was suddenly so buoyant.

"I'm picking out the clubs you'll need today," she said, not noticing or looking up. "Putter, five iron, seven iron, nine iron, driver." She stuck the clubs back into the bag and pushed the others aside.

"I have my own set, see?" Adam said, gesturing to the bag slung over his shoulder.

"You can leave them here," said Leela.

"But I need more than five clubs. What about the sand wedge?" Adam said, trying not to break his good mood.

"You won't be in the sand today," said Leela.

Adam felt doubt creeping in. He said, "I have two favorite putters, you know, and a couple of drivers with different graphite shafts."

"Lee Trevino won the 1974 PGA Championship with a putter he found in the attic," Leela said crisply. She thrust the bag of clubs at Adam and flicked on the switch. The rear wall of the vision simulator lit up with a scene Adam had dreamed about. Pebble Beach! He felt a rush. "We're playing there?" he asked.

"We're setting the course record," Leela said casually. "Should be a big day."

Feeling excited again, Adam was ready to attack the legendary course. But before he could take a step, Leela jerked his elbow. "This is going to go by pretty fast," she said. "I'll tell you the lesson first, so neither of us forgets."

I bet you never forget anything, thought Adam.

"Nothing is more important than now," said Leela, putting an emphasis on the last word. "Find the now, and you'll find the shot."

"I don't get it. It's always now," Adam pointed out.

"You think so?" said Leela. "A lot of the time it's soon. And when it's not soon, it's later. Wait long enough, and it may be never."

"Oh, I see," said Adam, half-humoring her. He didn't see how this advice was going to give him the perfect swing she'd promised. "I'll ponder that. But we still get to play Pebble Beach?"

Rather than answering, the next moment Leela was adjusting his shoulders and hips over the first tee. Adam gazed at the wide fairway that bent right with dangerous bunkers and trees to trap anyone who tried to bomb a driver off the tee. No problem. He didn't hit bombs, ever.

"I'm ready," he mumbled, not daring to look toward the clubhouse for fear of seeing spectators.

"Good, but you'll need this," said Leela. She held in her hand a small white cube with a red dome on top. She placed it on the ground at his feet a few inches from the tee. "Hit the ball when the light goes on."

"Why?" asked Adam.

"Because we're going to break the course record, and you'll want to do your part." Leela pointed to the red light, which was still dark, and Adam waited.

"Do I get any kind of warning?" he asked after a few seconds of nothing happening.

"No warning," said Leela. "Just hit the ball when the light goes on."

Within three seconds the red light was lit, and Adam took a swing. But instead of feeling the crisp contact with the ball, his driver passed through empty air. He looked down. The ball had disappeared.

"You missed," said Leela.

"I swung when I saw the light. Isn't that what you told me to do?" said Adam.

"I told you to hit the ball when you see the light," Leela replied. "That's different."

"You're kidding. I have to make contact at the same instant that a little red light goes on?" wailed Adam. "With no warning? It's impossible."

"You're right," said Leela. "It's impossible if you try to anticipate now, because now is now."

Adam felt incredibly frustrated. "It'll never work."

"We'll see," said Leela, already stepping off the tee. With Adam in tow, she found his ball in the middle of the fairway just past the bunkers on the left. It was perfectly placed for a short iron to the green. Adam stared.

Leela held up the white box. "Next shot," she said.

Adam wasn't even interested in trying; he felt she was toying with him. But the grandeur of the setting and the thought of more such vistas to come made him step up to the ball. He swung seemingly at random, and this time the red light went on just a fraction of a second before he made contact. He felt his club lightly brush the ball, which flew in a high arc, held for a second at apex, and fell onto the green. Adam couldn't see quite where. He had the impression that whatever swing he had made, it didn't really affect the shot.

When they walked up to the green, his ball was 3 feet from the hole. "Great," he muttered. "Why not just have it go in?"

"We don't need eighteen eagles to break the course record," replied Leela.

Despite his disgruntlement, Adam decided to try. He waited over his putt until he felt the urge to putt, and when he did, the putter face made contact precisely when the light went on. After a short straight roll, the ball found the center of the cup, and despite himself, Adam felt good.

As the next holes unfolded with the ocean coming into view, Adam contended with ravines and trees, yawning bunkers and undulating greens. His ball sailed past every obstacle, and the birdies piled up. He kept attempting to find the instant of perfect contact. The closer he got, the more confident he felt, but none of the shots really felt like his.

He stood with Leela looking out over the bay from the perch of the seventh tee. A hundred yards down the cliff, Adam spotted a patch of green no more than 60 feet across with rocks and surf growling on three sides. He felt queasy.

"I don't have this shot," he said.

"Maybe you don't, but it's there," Leela said. "And if you meet it, the shot will be yours." Leela's voice didn't sound as if she was trying to mystify him; she just sounded certain. So Adam addressed the ball and decided to apply what he knew already: be of one mind and let the swing happen.

That's when he felt it—the little red light gave a warning after all—a faint presence, a tiny wave of anticipation that triggered Adam's muscles. Without thought he took the club away and met the ball perfectly. He was so absorbed that he heard no crack at impact. His whole being stayed with the ball, becoming a point of complete stillness vanishing into limitless sky before turning back and allowing the earth to reclaim it, not like a rock plunging to the ground but like a child returning to its mother out of sheer, joyful desire. The intensity of these feelings swept over Adam so rapidly that he couldn't breathe. Nor could he quite hold on. Instead of dropping into the cup, his ball skirted the hole, rimmed it swiftly, and stopped 2 feet to the left.

"Wow," Adam murmured when he could breathe again. "So that's what a perfect shot feels like."

"That's what *now* feels like," said Leela. "But I had to trick you a little."

"You did? How?" asked Adam.

"I turned off the light for that one."

So the shot really had been his. Adam was speechless, fighting the swelling sensation in his chest, afraid to believe what he'd just done. Leela looked so pleased that Adam feared he wouldn't be allowed to finish the round. Usually Leela didn't linger when one of her lessons sank in, but this time, perhaps because of the idyllic day and the unforgettable setting, she relented.

Playing the Game

The third lesson is about the present moment. It can be summarized in one sentence: Now doesn't happen fast, it happens deep. To find the now, you have to plunge into it; skimming over the surface will not release the mysterious powers hidden in every moment.

An action that takes full advantage of the present involves three steps:

Diving deep into yourself.
Holding still when you get there.
Doing what you need to do.

When you dive deep, you access the power to organize your action and carry it through with maximum intelligence and coordination. When you hold still, you achieve focus and concentration. When you perform an action in that stillness, cause and effect are linked without a gap, flowing fluidly together.

The great Eastern sages say that these three steps all have spiritual significance:

Diving deep is meditation.
Holding still is one-pointed awareness.
Doing what you need to do is spontaneous right
    action.

When I was on the golf course, I couldn't help noticing that every once in a while I played beyond my abilities. I would be stuck in a bunker with a downhill lie, for example, which is one of the demon shots in golf. Even a good player can expect disaster here. If the ball is topped, always a danger when your feet are above the ball, it might ricochet off the lip of the bunker and never get out. If you hit the ball fat in an effort to compensate for the bad lie, a lot of sand gets between the club and the ball, resulting in a chunked shot.

Yet every so often, neither of these occurred. I swung and the ball sailed up and out of the sand, landing near the spot I had visualized. What made the difference? I realized that it was me. I was coming from a different place. I came from deep enough that three elements coincided: a larger intelligence could take over from my modest abilities; I could stay in that place without distraction; I could let the swing come about as it wanted to.

Taken all together, this process is known as Samyama. In golf, Samyama occurs whenever a player finds the shot. Timing, rhythm, sequence, and power all come together as if by magic. The swing becomes more than the sum of its parts. Of course, it is important to make the parts as good as you can. Body memory needs something to work with. But diving into the present moment and holding still while letting the action occur is the secret to extraordinary execution.

When you begin losing the now, you feel vaguely uncomfortable. Although your mechanics might be proceeding fairly well, something indefinable is not quite right. As the pros say, you can't find your swing. Drifting further out of the present moment brings disastrous results:

Your body goes off-balance.
The timing of the shot is off.
You take your eye off the ball.
You lose the line of the putt.
Your weight no longer shifts easily and properly.
Parts of the body begin to lock up.

It's a trap to try and correct these symptoms one at a time, because they are connected. Yet the mind can't adjust all of them at once, either. (It is said that when a player is struggling to remember all the tips he's been taught about a model swing, no more than two can be held in the mind at the same time.)

The solution to finding the shot is to find the now.

Samyama works because there is deep intelligence in the region we call the subconscious. This is a terribly misleading name for the part of ourselves that is actually more conscious than any other part. The logical mind produces a sequence of ideas one at a time, strung like pearls on a string, but the unconscious is performing literally millions of functions with utmost precision. A hundred trillion cells in your body operate with perfect knowledge of what each is doing. In the brain itself, a simple task like lining up a 2-foot putt requires instant coordination of neurons in the visual cortex, along with input from the parts of the lower brain that control balance, motor coordination, and the delicate weaving of all these functions into one whole.

The whole exists already in the now.

In golf it's well known that thinking too much ruins the shot. What isn't often understood, however, is that thinking *itself* ruins the shot by blocking out the limitless abilities of the unconscious. Your ego-mind has been trained for years to stand between you and the present moment. Watch yourself the next time you face a long pressure putt. Notice how desperately your mind tries to avoid the shot. It dwells on minute details—the spike marks on the green, the distracting sounds of birds and squirrels. It might drift off into fantasy or concern about what your partner is going to say. Visions of failure flit through your imagination. Anticipated humiliation (or, for that matter, triumph) block what lies before you now. If the pressure is wicked enough, you might start to see things. One player recounted that he often saw dirt or an insect on the ball, a sure sign that his nerves had caved.

All these distractions are attempts by your ego-mind to preserve its dominance. A long putt can't be controlled, however. It only makes sense to call upon those powers that might contribute to the shot. Yet the conscious mind refuses to give up its authority. This stubbornness disguises itself as logic, trying to convince you that if you just remember enough tips, talk to yourself positively, and push aside all distractions, everything will work. It mostly won't, because logic is out of its depth here. The wisdom of the body isn't linear, it is holistic. You can no more think your way through a golf swing than you can think your way through a triple somersault off a high diving board.

You will be approaching the now once you have absorbed the lessons about being of one mind and letting the swing happen. But there's more to learn, beginning with how to relax. Tension blocks the flow of information from the unconscious. Freezing with fear is an extreme example— there is so much tightness in the body that it can't remember the most basic movements. Being far more intricate than most moves, a golf swing demands as much relaxation as you can bring to it. (I don't have to stress how many golfers, amateur and professional alike, are bedeviled by memories of bad shots that live on as tension in the body that impairs the ability to swing with anything like a natural rhythm. Watching someone's swing fall apart is almost as painful as having it happen to yourself.)

Relaxation is actually a profound spiritual secret. In India a huge emphasis is placed on finding what is called "the subtle breath" as the road to the soul. How can this be? We all take breathing for granted. The secret is that breathing is like an entire book distilled into one sentence—it contains the essence of everything your cells are doing. For every state of mind there is a state of breath, and if you want to find the deeper levels of mind and body, your next breath is a more reliable guide than your next thought, because thoughts can deceive you into thinking all is well; you can't hide fear and discomfort from your breathing.

In a very simple sense, breathing is also valuable because it sends its message now. You can hold back your thoughts for days or weeks or years at a time before you face them, and the same is true for emotions. At most you can hold your breath only a few minutes. Your golf swing can't be postponed beyond a few minutes either. There is far too much intricacy in the golf swing to calculate it in advance. Only in the now will you find exactly what you are able to give to the shot. In fact, the deeper you dive, past the tension and resistance, the more natural—the more like yourself—you will feel. Chaos and anxiety are very superficial layers of reality. Life wants to be orderly. How else could DNA have preserved its unbelievably complex organization for billions of years, adding new details through the passage of time while losing none? When Jesus declared, "Knock and the door shall be opened," He was indicating how effortless it is to enter the now. Once you know that the door is open, you know how to reach mastery. Dive as deep as you can, hold yourself in stillness, perform the action at hand. All of this happens in the now, and when it happens perfectly, the result is a miracle.

Time is the gift of moments that never end. Living in the perpetual now makes eternity possible.

Applied to Life

Whatever can be done to remove trapped energy is always valuable. Trapped energy is a general term for the body's ability to hold on to old thoughts, feelings, reactions, and memories that have not yet been resolved. These keep us from living in the now the way layers of varnish keep us from seeing an old painting as the master intended it.

Unlike trapped water or coal, which remains unusable as long as it is underground, trapped energy affects us from its emotional hiding place. It taps out warnings of danger and anxiety that cannot be ignored. Since anxiety is the most common emotion that the body holds on to, because it is the most difficult to face, we will concentrate on it. In life as in golf, diving through the dark pockets of fear is the direct road to finding your center.

Sit comfortably. Become aware of your breathing until it begins to quiet down. Now, slowly draw a deeper breath, feeling it dip into your stomach. Do this gradually, taking in your breath until it seems to hit an obstacle. You will immediately recognize the moment, because you will feel a sudden need to exhale. Go ahead and do that. Release your breath with a sigh, feeling the relief that comes naturally. Don't force the sigh, just see yourself letting go of one pebble in a pile or the top layer in a pool of water.

With the next breath, go a little deeper into the pit of your stomach. When you feel resistance, accompanied by the need to exhale, again release your breath with a sigh. Do this systematically, drawing air from below the stomach, reaching into your intestines, lower abdomen, pubic bone, and down your legs to your feet. Take as much time as you need. Go as deep as you can. If you run out of time or feel too much resistance, stop. Don't push your breathing further. Even one or two breaths will be doing you quite a lot of good in releasing trapped energy. Feel your shoulders dip and your neck relax. Notice the knots of stress appearing where you never noticed them before. This is cause for congratulations—you are accessing tensions that want to be recognized and released.

Anyone can achieve deeper and deeper levels of relaxation. Once you do, you automatically unravel the energy of fear. Forget the content of fear—the story it is telling you—with its countless images of horrible outcomes. When the trapped energy departs with your breath, these images must follow. Anxiety is so uncomfortable that it's natural for the mind to try to find a way to live with it, and it does so by stuffing it down into trapped energy. (As Freud once said, fear is like an unwelcome guest who won't leave the house, therefore one has to pretend that it is a friend.)

After breathing comes paying attention. What is your body saying? Every energy wants you to know something, and until you pay attention, it won't fully go away. Most people hate the feeling of anxiety so much that the last thing they want to do is listen to it. You can ease yourself past this defense by knowing that your fears want to depart. They can only do so once they have successfully performed their job, which is to let you know that some part of you feels wounded and weak. This wound was created in the past. Where you have healed, it feels strong and confident; where you have not, it feels weak and fearful.

Wounds are made in the past but healed in the present.

Having opened up to any trapped energy, ask for it to be healed. You can do this by applying the strongest power of the mind: forgiveness. Everyone is ashamed of being weak, but when you understand, accept, and then release any old energy, you have achieved forgiveness.

This breathing sequence is advisable any time you feel nervous. Anxiety infects the whole game of life, and so there will be countless opportunities to release this particular energy. As you do so you will change your whole reality, not just your golf swing.

The deeper you go, the better your life will be.

It's a spiritual law that silence, order, intelligence, and creativity come from deep levels of the self. Using the steps you've now learned, take advantage of this spiritual law.

LESSON 4

*

Play from Your Heart to the Hole

Adam walked away from his last lesson with a strange sensation. It was as if time had melted away. Work came and went. He took an out-of-town trip to visit one of his accounts. Yet none of these things seemed to take any time. Standing still and moving began to be less distinct. He remembered something Leela had said: "The now never ends because it never began."

Then one day he had to interact with Doris, the office dragon. "You dated this report for the wrong year," she shouted the moment she entered the door. "Don't you know how that screws up the cumulative stats?" The rasp in Doris's voice came from years of cigarettes and whiskey. "You're supposed to be smart, but a smart guy knows the difference between a calendar year and a fiscal year, right?"

She stood with hands on hips, staring down at Adam with a face toughened by decades of office combat. As always, he tried not to meet her eyes. Everyone prayed for the day when Doris left the company and took her accumulated misery and anger with her, but she kept postponing her retirement year after year.

"The date was right when it left here," Adam mumbled. "Maybe you copied it wrong." He felt a wave of wrath smack him from across the desk.

"Let me tell you this, buddy—" Doris barked. Despite himself, Adam looked up. He faced the bulldog jowls and steely eyes he expected, but they became transparent, and through them Adam saw a carefree child, a curious adolescent, a loving young woman. All of them were still there, hidden under the mask that Doris showed the world. Time had buried them.

Adam saw something else just as clearly. Time wasn't his enemy anymore. Each day wasn't given to him only to be snatched away at nightfall. Every possibility in life lay open to him, layer upon layer, in the now.

"Adam?" said Doris. In his amazement he must have zoned out her tirade. For some reason Doris's voice had calmed down. "I could have copied it wrong. Let me check, and I'll let you know," she said, then turned and left almost meekly.

What happened? Adam thought. He hadn't treated Doris any differently this time, yet her response was nothing less than miraculous. Then he knew. He had seen these aspects of Doris she kept hidden from the world, and somehow she knew that he had. To see someone that way, you have to step out of time. And he had done just that.

It astonished him that merely seeing something was enough to change everything. Leela knew this. She was trying to get Adam to see himself entirely differently, to see the ball and the shot and the hole in a new way. With innocence, one might say. So far this was happening in fits and starts— but it was happening. Now all Adam wanted was to find the secret for staying in the now. After taming Doris, why not his own dragons?

The next morning happened to be the day of his lesson. He jumped into the car and backed out of the driveway at top speed. If he hadn't taken a second glance into his side mirror, he would have driven right over Leela.

"You?" he said incredulously. Adam was certain he had not seen anyone when he started the car. Dressed in her usual white shirt and blue shorts, Leela got into the passenger's side. She glanced at Adam from beneath her visor.

"Don't worry, you'll get your lesson," she said, apparently reading his mind. "Your motor's running."

Adam put the car in gear. Instead of heading for the old dirt road, Leela directed him to the local public golf course. Adam had played there as a kid, although once he had the means he had quickly switched to the country club.

"So, no vision simulator today?" he said, more than a little disappointed.

"No vision at all," said Leela without explanation.

Near the first tee Adam saw a motley bunch of teenagers with boom boxes, a foursome of twenty-somethings in T-shirts with six-packs of beer strapped on to their cart. Off to the side stood a lone figure.

"Him," Leela said, pointing. Once they drew near, the solitary figure, a man in his forties, turned around.

"Are you my caddie?" he asked.

"He is," said Leela. "And I'm here to teach you."

"I don't need a teacher," the man said.

"I agree," said Leela. The man laughed and faced Adam.

"Did you know that the word *caddie* comes from the French word *cadet,* or *military cadet?*"

"No, I didn't," said Adam. Leela nodded, and he hesitantly took the man's bag. The man, who said his name was Parker, was looking at a point 3 inches to the left of Adam's face as he talked. He was blind.

"The wind's okay now," Parker said. "It was swirling before, but this time of day it tends to die down."

He reached out and felt for his clubs, pulling out the two iron by touch. "I like to start off with this one. My woods want to hook, so this gives me more confidence off the first tee."

Adam nodded, then realized Parker couldn't see him. "Good idea," he said. He watched as Leela took Parker and lined him up square to the target. Without touching the ball with his club head, Parker wiggled the head in the right vicinity until Leela said, "You've got it." Parker's body relaxed. He held the club at the address position for a second, then drew it back slowly, pausing slightly at the top of the backswing. With a gliding motion in his hips and a smooth torque of the shoulders, he made good contact. The ball flew in a straight line down the heart of the fairway.

"Not bad," he said.

"Want me to tell you where it landed?" asked Adam.

"It felt like a hundred and fifty yards," Parker said.

"Pretty close," said Adam. "Maybe a hundred and eighty."

"Yes," the blind man said. "I heard it and felt it. Sometimes I think you can even smell a good shot."

Parker was very cheerful. Without waiting to be led away, he strode off the tee. Adam slung the bag over his back and followed, wondering what Leela would do next.

An angel's going to make your day.

Nothing magical happened, however. It was miracle

enough that Parker played as well as he did. His second shot on the par 4 almost made the green. He screwed up his face.

"Short for me, but like I said, I begin with a bit of nerves."

Adam couldn't help thinking that blind golf seemed rather pointless, without the benefit of seeing your ball in flight, being able to take in the beautiful scenery, or judging the lie of the putting surface. But as he walked around the course, he realized that he was wrong on all counts. Parker loved being out on the course and expressed appreciation for the pure air, the rustling wind, and the shimmer of trees that reached him without being seen. He had a real feeling for the ball in flight that began with the *crack* made at contact.

Adam expected the downfall in Parker's game to be putting. He couldn't conceive of reading a green without seeing it. But Leela needed only to line up the putt and explain it to him, and Parker got amazingly close each time.

Parker must have sensed Adam's puzzlement. "Think about facing a putt," he said. "If it's longer than a couple of feet, you can't see the ball and the hole at the same time. One or the other has to fall outside your field of vision. A lot of players miss short putts because their eyes dart back and forth to the cup. But a good putt only has to be right for the first six inches. If you have the line and the distance, those first few inches determine everything that follows, right? No one can control the ball once it leaves the putter."

Parker shot forty-two on the front nine. Adam, who had

often done a lot worse, took Leela aside. "He's amazing, isn't he?" he whispered.

"Yes, he is," said Leela. "Want to try it?"

Before Adam could reply, Leela touched his forehead lightly with one fingertip, and Adam's sight faded to black. As much as he trusted Leela, his heart nearly jumped out of his chest with apprehension. "Just for a moment," said Leela close to his ear. "You have already learned how to see the ball. Now we'll take it further. Don't try to see anything. Calm down, then listen to me."

Calming down didn't come quickly. Adam had no idea where they were; he knew only that Parker was no longer there. Rather than worrying about this, he peered into darkness and tried to imagine it as a velvety night without stars or the inside of a warm cave.

"That's better," said Leela. "Here, I'm putting a nine iron in your hands."

The familiar wound grip of a golf club calmed Adam down. His heartbeat, which had sounded like a roar in his ears, faded.

Leela said, "We're a hundred and ten yards from the green. It's right in front of you with a little elevation in the front. Try to aim over the flag, which is dead center."

Adam felt her hands positioning his shoulders and hips. "Where's the ball?" he asked, moving the club head around to find it.

"I'll put the ball down when you're ready. The green slopes sharply to the right, and there's sand on the left. Got that?"

"Are you going to put down a ball now?" Adam asked.

"No. Just swing. If you do it right, you'll know where the ball is going," Leela said.

Air golf, Adam thought to himself. He swung carelessly, wondering what Leela expected.

"Where did it go?" she asked.

"Nowhere," said Adam, "unless you can tell me."

"Whether I know or not won't get the shot to the green," she said. "Try again."

Adam tried harder the second time. He visualized the scene Leela had painted for him: slightly elevated green that sloped right with bunkers on the left. Taking the club back in a half-swing, he chopped downward to make it fly up, hopefully in a high arc that would plunk into a soft landing without much roll.

Leela was silent. "It's not going where you want it to," she finally said.

"Really? I don't know what I'm doing, and I can't see a thing. Does that make it harder?"

"You think I've made it tough for you?" asked Leela. "This is a game of touch. At the end of the 2000 season at Akron, rain delays stretched out the final round. Coming to the last hole, Tiger Woods had a shot to the green that was in almost total darkness. The only illumination was from flashlights and butane lighters held up by the spectators. The ball went over a hundred and fifty yards and landed inches from the cup."

"And you expect me to make the same shot, only without flashlights," Adam grumbled. He surprised himself with his sarcasm. Why was this so hard for him?

"Keep trying, and don't talk until you hit the ball," Leela replied crisply.

Adam swung again without enthusiasm. A few shots later he started to get frustrated, which led to being angry. It was stupid that he could get so enraged trying to hit an invisible ball, but he kept thinking that he was missing it. Strange. A dozen strokes later he wasn't angry anymore. He felt defeated. After a bit this turned into feeling alone and abandoned. What was going on? He would have given up on this preposterous exercise, but one mood led to the next. He moved through feeling awkward, weak, embarrassed, and incompetent.

"Am I getting anywhere? I want to quit," he said. Leela didn't respond, so he kept swinging. Half an hour passed. Now he was angry again, and then he realized something. If he kept it up, the same feelings were going to come around, like horses on a merry-go-round. He would experience the whole thing all over again. All because of a ball that wasn't even there. Adam stopped.

"I didn't hit the hole yet, but I found out something," he announced.

"You haven't gotten to the green yet," Leela corrected him.

Adam plowed on. "What I found out is this: Being blind can make you see what's really going on," said Adam. It was true. The circling horses on the merry-go-round had always been there. He had never really played a whole game without them, but now he had become aware of them for the first time.

"Good." Leela's voice had softened. "Those feelings block your game because they block your touch. Get out of your head. Go where touch begins. Play from your heart to the hole."

Then the darkness in Adam's head really did become like a night sky without stars. He drew back the club, not in a breezy half-swing, but with conviction. Just as Parker had said, Adam felt the ball leave the club face. He heard the sound of solid contact and saw the high trajectory of the ball. All his senses came together into one.

"Close," he muttered. He knew where the invisible ball had landed, on the front skirt of the green.

He hit the next ball the same distance but a little closer to the cup. The third went over the flag then rolled back within a foot of the hole.

"Now, that one I'd be proud of," Leela said admiringly. She was right there with him.

Her encouragement must have been what he needed. On

the next shot Adam never left the ball. It flew as true as his best friend and poured into the hole with barely 2 feet of roll.

"I want to hit a real one now. Put the ball down," he whispered.

"I already did," said Leela. She touched his forehead again with her fingertip, and Adam felt himself dazzled by the sunlight flooding his eyes.

"Just the last time?" he asked. "I heard a crack at impact every time."

"Just the last time," said Leela. "The others were imaginary."

Adam's eyesight cleared. He looked up at the green, which was just as Leela had described it. The putting surface was empty and smooth.

"So if there's one ball up there," said Adam, "it's in the hole."

"Right," Leela said. "You want to go pick it up?"

Adam thought a second. "No need," he smiled. "Let's go find Parker and finish his round."

Playing the Game

The fourth lesson is about intuition. Intuition tells you exactly what is right when nothing else can. Although most people consider intuition less reliable than logic and therefore do not call upon its power, golf is one sport in which intuition plays a major role. It is the key to a mysterious factor called "touch."

On a 12-foot putt, the range that makes or breaks many tournaments, the player who has lost his touch will consistently miss the hole by a few inches or maybe less than that, whereas the player who has touch sinks the ball time after time. Practice isn't what makes the difference, for a golf professional following the same routine as always might find his touch one week and lose it the next. Where, then, does touch come from?

Spiritual teachers locate touch not in the hands or even the head. They assign it to the subtle body, which in Sanskrit is called *sukshma sharira*. Your subtle body is the self you inhabit on the outer fringe of the physical realm. You take it into dreams and fantasies. Its specialty is insight; its energy is inspiration. If I ask you to close your eyes and visualize yourself walking through every room in your house, it's your subtle body that does it. Some people are deeply acquainted with their subtle bodies and therefore use them with incredible skill.

One example of this is blind golfers, of whom there are more than just a few. They can master a very straight swing, because blind golfers are not distracted by the visual cues that make a player push or pull his drive. The top players among the blind routinely break ninety, their shots being lined up by their caddies. When one of these caddies was asked if he saw any particular advantage that blind golfers might have, he replied that they benefit from not seeing the hazards on the course—in fact, if there was water in play, he sometimes didn't inform the player, just to relieve him of the jittery nerves that dunk so many balls.

If you can align with your subtle senses, you will have found the secret of touch.

Your subtle senses are closer to the source of intelligence. Have you ever been looking for a lost object, such as car keys or your wallet, when all of a sudden you know with certainty where it is? I can remember walking out of my house one spring as the snow was melting. Spontaneously my head swiveled left. My eyes fell automatically on a patch of lawn just emerging from its winter blanket, and I saw a tiny, barely perceptible object no one would think to look for. I picked it up and instantly recognized it as a tortoise-shell button that had fallen off my favorite coat. It had lain under the snow for three months waiting for my subtle body to spot it.

One of the best ways to get aligned with your subtle body is through visualization. Many professionals pause to see their shots in advance of making them. They visualize the trajectory they want on the ball along with the exact distance and roll when it lands. Many accomplished professionals play their entire round in advance. Such visualization isn't just imagination. It connects one's physical eyes with one's much sharper subtle eyes.

Let's take this a step further. Neurologists have discovered that certain parts of the body occupy much more space in the brain than others; this is called their cortical representation. For example, in your cortex your hands occupy a huge space compared to your legs, arms, or feet. What this tells us is that the subtle body has not just huge hands but extremely refined touch. Imagine running your fingers over velvet, then over a peach. Velvet and peach fuzz are much alike, yet to our hands they each have a completely unique signature.

This degree of refinement enters into your putting. Well-manicured greens look about the same, yet each one has its own degree of firmness, slope, grain, undulation, and pace. Like faces, no two greens are exactly alike. The next time you have to make a putt, crouch and pretend to feel the texture of the surface with your flattened palms. Now, leaving your hands in place, move your subtle hands an inch forward and pretend to feel the grass with them.

Next, move your subtle hands back into alignment with your physical hands. Then have them go out again, only a bit farther this time. Do this repeatedly (a practice green is recommended, naturally, since you can't usually take as much time as needed for this exercise during a round). Even practicing on your front lawn is good.

The object is to trust your subtle hands enough that they can feel the putting surface the way you can feel the fuzz of a peach. Starting with a few inches, some players eventually find themselves able to feel the whole distance of the putt. Combined with a good visual read, your sense of subtle touch will add to your ability to assess distance and direction in one smooth moment.

Another exercise is simpler and takes less time. Take your stance and swing with your favorite driver just as you would in taking a practice swing before teeing off. Experience the swing as natural and comfortable. Feel what it's like when the club head hits the ball square. Do this a few times, then take your swing with your subtle body only, leaving the club at address.

Put as much power into the subtle swing as you would if the club actually moved. Use touch and sight together, but mainly touch. Feel yourself gripping the club and driving its weight around into a complete follow-through. Hold the pose at the end until you can feel the weight of the club head. Repeat this exercise, first with a physical swing, then a subtle swing. Try swinging them together, then separating them again. Almost anyone can feel his or her subtle swing the first time out, and as you get good at it, you will be able to align your subtle swing with your real swing much better.

When insight is added to sight, you double your game.

The subtle body is your second body, operating at the periphery of every cell and fiber. This second body never ages. All that you were as a child is present in its memory, along with all that you will become. The desires of yesterday are filed there, along with the knowledge of whether they came true. The desires you don't yet know about but that time will unfold are waiting there to be born. You navigate through time with a part of yourself that lives just on the brink of the timeless. The best navigators understand this and take advantage. Like subtle hands feeling the green and inching forward, their minds have a feeling for the next step, the next choice, the next solution. The subtle body has been sent ahead like a scout to discover the lay of the future.

Here golf reflects life perfectly. Subtle eyes can make impossible shots come true, not by magic but by calling upon a new layer of reality. If that is so, what is to keep your subtle body from taking you into new possibilities that you already see and only need to follow?

Applied to Life

People are wary of intuition without knowing that at least once in their lives it played the dominant role. This is the case when you fall in love. How do you know someone is "the right one"? What accounts for sensations that seem completely new and powerful surging up from an invisible region? This is all the action of the subtle body. Your subtle body, as the name implies, is easily trampled on by the gross body. The push and shove of ego bullies the subtler senses into obedience. Love disarms this dynamic. Because you desire to be as close to the beloved as possible, you become egoless for a blissful time, usually all too short. Then ego asserts itself once more, and the subtle body goes back into hiding.

To welcome those experiences that filter through the sieve of timelessness—love, ecstasy, inspiration, prophecy, clairvoyance—your subtle body must be open. Here are some ways to nurture it:

Trust what you feel over what you think.

Discount strong, pushy feelings like anger, resentment, greed, hatred, envy, jealousy, and selfishness. These never come from the subtle body; they mask it.

Day by day, give your intuition a little more to work with. Let your hunches be your guide, trust instinct, override your fears and apprehensions with trust.

Don't trust blindly. Give your allegiance to the best outcome that you can truly see and truly desire. What many people loosely call "following your dream" is actually a matter of trusting your subtle perception and where it wants to lead you.

Finally, learn to recognize the egoless state. It is easy, carefree, open, yet alert and attuned. As with falling in love, you can't describe the feeling, but once you've experienced it, the hallmarks are unmistakable. Unlike falling in love, being free of your ego can be achieved many times every day. Each time you notice yourself in a clear space, acknowledge it and tell yourself that this is how you wish to exist more and more.

LESSON 5

✳

Winning Is Passion with Detachment

✳ The next day, Adam had the queer sensation of feeling the world as much as seeing it. Not exactly the whole world, just a part he couldn't name. At odd moments he turned around expecting to see somebody when no one was there. He thought he felt a tickle at the back of his neck like a hovering gnat, but when he slapped at it he hit only air.

The spookiest part came at night. He turned over in bed toward the big window at the end of the room. The gauze curtains fluttered in; a faint breeze. Adam sat bolt upright. He always kept that window shut.

"Who are you?" he called out, still half-asleep. This was an automatic reaction, the kind that happens before your brain has a chance to catch up. When Adam did come fully awake, there was no one there. But he wasn't fooled by this vanishing act. Someone was definitely interested in him.

Two days later, while doing nothing, Adam sensed the air wrapping itself around his body like the ocean swirling around a sailing ship. In the air was a pleasant stream of energy. This also shaped itself around his body, and he thought, *So it doesn't just want to watch. It wants to touch me.*

If he'd been a different person, someone who had never met Leela, his skin would have crawled, but the energy was so pleasant that Adam felt a sense of loss when it began fading away. *Wait,* he called unconsciously. But it wouldn't. It had touched him and now wanted to leave.

I'm doing something wrong, Adam thought instantly, seizing on the last wisps to try to keep them from departing. He looked around. He had been watching the evening news, something about a war far away. On instinct he changed the channel. He felt the wispy energy flicker a little, as if it wanted to return.

I understand, he thought. It didn't like violence. He punched the remote and found a station rerunning old comedies. No, the energy was still fading away near the vanishing point now. So Adam jumped up and ran outside, where the summer evening was merging into the oncoming darkness. An orange cusp of the sun lingered like a sliver on the horizon. Adam felt the energy pausing as shyly as a young girl before a kiss. The more still Adam became, the more it wanted him.

"I understand," Adam said, this time talking to the energy. He looked up. High cirrus clouds in shades of pink and orange ran from the horizon to the zenith of the sky like banners painted for a parade in heaven. The moment he gazed up, the energy swelled and became like a caress.

If only you would stay, Adam thought. Actually it was a kind of wistful prayer, a prayer born of doubt. The energy disappeared, leaving one last tickle at the back of his neck. Adam didn't slap at it.

Golf is golf, he thought, *but this is something else.*

There was nothing to be done until he went to the shack. That evening he went to bed with a haunting memory; he woke up the next morning with a desire that turned to yearning; and by Saturday he wondered how he had ever lived without the mysterious stranger who had so briefly touched him.

For the first time, Leela was waiting at the door of the shack. "Your hair is sticking up," she remarked. "Did you sleep on it wrong?"

"Are you playing with me? What was it?" Adam asked. His eyes were dark and wild with lack of sleep.

"You said you didn't want to turn back," Leela reminded him. "Or words to that effect. So somebody heard you."

✳

"Tell me what happened," said Adam, unable to control his irritation.

"Congratulations. You met what is," said Leela, then nothing more.

Adam was so jumpy he could have screamed. In fact, his agitation was increasing exponentially, and he had no idea why. "What is 'what is'?" he asked.

"That's a strange-sounding question, don't you think?" Leela was sounding amiable. "You might as well ask what is what *isn't*. Most people have a very good idea of what is not." She courteously opened the door to the shack, as if she expected her remark to be the end of it. Adam calmed down a trifle. He had learned that Leela became mischievous to get his attention.

She went on, "What is has a presence. You felt it approaching."

"I thought someone was watching me," said Adam.

"Right. Then you began to pay attention, and what is came closer."

"It wanted to touch me," Adam explained, and the faint memory of its caress made him shiver.

Leela shook her head. "No, it didn't want to touch you. It didn't want to watch you, either. You created that."

"But it did," Adam protested. His voice rose in fear that Leela was going to take this wonderful thing away.

"What is doesn't want anything," said Leela. "You're getting upset because you think it comes and goes. You're preparing yourself for losing it, because it has taken you so long to find it again."

Leela's normally light tone had become grave. Adam felt emotion welling up inside. Rather than look at him, Leela turned away and mused out loud. "People suffer in the most remarkable way because they try to get out of what is into what is not."

"Explain," Adam murmured softly, or perhaps he just thought it.

Leela looked up as if interested in the branches of a half-withered tree. "When you're in the present, you're in the presence. But that doesn't happen too often. You leap around a lot."

"Why do I do that?" said Adam, regaining some composure.

Leela darted a glance at him. She must have been satisfied, because her tone grew light again. "Okay. Here's what happens. You don't get something you really, really want. You can relate to that." She put it out as a statement rather than a question. Adam felt his face grow hot.

Leela went on. "The feeling of not getting what you want hurts. It also reminds you of how insecure you feel most of the time. If you think about it, not getting what you want has been happening a lot. Too much. So instead of just feeling the pain of not getting what you want, you build up defenses against losing again. You fantasize. You run away in advance. You go for successes that don't mean anything compared to the ones you think you can never have. All that stuff is unreal. It's what is not. It makes you feel better for a while, but it always turns out to be a fake."

"What about the energy? Where does it come from?" asked Adam.

"No one can say. Maybe it's our prize for being in the game," said Leela.

Adam nodded, but he wondered if he'd ever feel that wonderful sensation again. His attempt to put on a good face made Leela burst out laughing. "Don't look so hangdog. You didn't lose a loved one."

"Who says?" mumbled Adam.

"You're right," she said more gently. "The reason we love anyone is to get a taste of what is. That's why falling in love feels more real than anything else—and why falling out of love feels like the passing of a mirage. You can't pretend to be in the presence once it's gone."

"How do I get back there?" Adam asked.

"That's what you're learning all the time," she said.

This time Adam accepted her invitation to walk into the shack. Leela's explanations always had the effect of making him feel better.

Perhaps because he still looked a bit shaky, Leela didn't turn on the lights. The afternoon sun fell in patches on the plank floor of the shack. She found a bright spot and set down a portable metal cup for putting. Adam had one in his desk just like it in case he wanted to practice at the office.

"Okay," Leela said. "Let's try a really hard one."

She put a golf ball down some 18 inches from the cup. "Think you're up to it?" she asked.

As usual, Adam didn't understand. But instead of walking into her scheme, whatever it was, he hit the ball into the cup. Leela picked it up and replaced it in the same spot.

"Again," she told him. "And remember, this is going to be the hardest shot of your life. Don't take it casually."

Adam's curiosity was aroused, but he couldn't find a way to make the putt tough, much less the hardest shot of his life. He sank the 18-incher and stood up.

"So now I do this a hundred times and the light dawns," he said, smiling. He knew the drill.

"Just one more time," Leela said. Before Adam could address the putt, however, she flicked on the lights. He heard a murmuring crowd and saw a marshal holding up a sign reading QUIET PLEASE. For a moment Adam was disoriented. He still had his putter in hand, but now he could sense many bodies pressed close around him. Four rows of spectators were blocking his view.

"You've brought me to a tournament?" he whispered to Leela, who was close beside him.

"Ssh," he heard a voice hiss behind him. What was he

supposed to see? Ahead of him was a solid row of backs. He felt tension in the air, then the crowd let out a moan. Another pause, and the same loud moan, only more distressed, went up.

Leela took him by the elbow. "Coming through," she called, pulling Adam to the front. Time seemed to freeze when they got there. Two golfers stood on the green, and one of them was bent over an 18-inch putt. Adam's putt. He felt a sickening lurch in his stomach.

Leela didn't bother to be quiet. "Eighteenth green of the U.S. Open. That one"—she pointed at the player who wasn't putting—"has just missed a 3-foot putt, but that one"—she pointed to the player bent over his putter—"has just missed, too. Everyone is shocked. He had a two-stroke lead. Now it's down to one."

"So if he misses this one," said Adam.

"Catastrophe," said Leela, finishing his sentence. Around them no one was moving. Adam and Leela had stepped out of time, it seemed. "It's just eighteen inches," Leela said.

But he's going to miss, thought Adam, knowing the worst.

"Not if we can help it."

Leela waved her hand toward a marshal, who trotted over. "We've got a substitute," she said.

"A what?" said the marshal.

"He's taking over the putt." Leela pushed Adam forward.

It was like a horrible dream. The marshal nodded, the man standing over the putt stepped aside, and Adam found himself in the sucking center of the universe, a universe where nothing in creation was as crucial as the shot he would make or miss.

"I can't do this," he hissed in Leela's direction. She didn't hear him. No one did. They were all waiting with bated breath for him to make the winning putt. Adam felt paralyzed, helpless to do anything but perform his assigned task. He drew the putter back, his eyes squeezed tight. He couldn't look at it; he just had to get the shot over with.

"Stop," said Leela. She was beside him now, holding back the club with her hand. No one moved.

"I'm about to screw this up," said Adam.

"Actually, you're not," said Leela, sounding amazingly relaxed.

"Really?"

"Absolutely."

Adam's trust was such that his lurching stomach and paralyzed nerves vanished. *God Almighty,* he thought. Now he couldn't wait to draw back the putter. He saw the crowd leaping up and down, the press rushing him. Leela held on to the club.

"Let go," he hissed.

She shook her head. "You want it to be you who wins, don't you?" she asked.

"It will be close enough if I sink this," Adam protested, feeling incredibly frustrated.

"You wish," said Leela. Adam didn't see her do anything, but suddenly the green was far away. He was out on the fairway striding toward it. His heart was pounding a thousand beats a minute; he could smell victory and it felt tremendous. But he wasn't Adam anymore.

My God, he realized. *I'm that guy.*

It was true. Leela had put him inside the player who thought he was going to win by two strokes. Adam felt the man's elation and the kick of adrenaline that made the ground float under his feet. Only on the very edge of his mind was there any suspicion that things were not going to turn out right.

He doesn't know yet, Adam realized. *He has no way of seeing what's coming.*

Adam felt himself walking onto the final green. The crowd roared in his ears. He felt the man salute the ovation, then glance over at his opponent. Then events unfolded. The 3-footer was missed.

This is unbelievable, Adam thought. He felt the man bend over the 18-inch putt that would settle the tournament. The air was completely silent, but Adam could feel the chaos of the man's emotions churning inside him. Every moment of his life seemed to flash by. The demon of failure rose up in all its fury, and the man fought against it. His mind swirled with hopeless reassurances. This is dead easy. This putt is practically a gimme.

Adam didn't want to stand by and watch. He wanted to change history and save this guy. But how? He might only make matters worse by adding his own intense desire. Then all at once Adam knew what to do. There was only one gift he could give a player who already had skill, determination, valor, and luck. Adam whispered in a silent voice, *Whether you win or lose is totally unknown. Stop trying to control the unknown.*

Adam wondered if he had been heard. The putter drew back, and Adam sensed the faintest change in the player's aim. The ball headed for the hole, but instead of rimming it, the ball sank into the heart of the cup, and the crowd sent up a collective roar to heaven.

Leela got Adam out of there instantly. They were back behind the crowd walking away, not joining in the hurrahs.

"You did it," Leela said with genuine appreciation.

"I didn't do much. I let him stand aside. He had everything else already," said Adam.

"He had the passion. You gave him the detachment," Leela remarked. "That's a lot more than anyone realizes."

Adam nodded. "It's a lot more than I ever realized."

Winning is passion with detachment. Adam knew he would remember this lesson as long as he lived.

Playing the Game

The fifth lesson is about power. There is a special kind of power that golf calls for, one that swings from unleashed might to delicate finesse in a matter of seconds. A big drive off the tee maximizes the largest muscle groups in the body. Once you step onto the putting surface, however, throttling down this output runs into obstacles: nerves, self-doubt, and uncertainty raise up bad memories of putts gone wrong, while at the physical level the body finds it hard to calm down when serenity is most needed.

In a way this is a glorious dilemma. The same power that runs the universe is coursing through you right now. In the softest shot using the lightest hands, you are commanding forces born in the Big Bang. The Indian spiritual masters must have known this, because they made life energy sacred and gave it the name Shakti. Life energy comes from the place inside yourself where peace passes understanding, as Jesus taught. It is the same place where all things can be accomplished, even moving mountains. This might sound very far removed from everyday life, but Shakti isn't. Its touch can be felt in a dozen ways, beginning with the soft, streaming energy we experience at peak moments or the certainty that comes at moments of clarity.

Golf is about energy control. On long drives, your energy

has to be unleashed or you will have some long second shots, making it tough to reach the green in regulation. On 10-foot putts, energy has to be reined in or you will run by the hole 5 feet. Instead of staying with the mind as it says, "I have to give this everything I've got" or "I have to barely touch the ball," you can go deeper, to that place where peace is married to power.

In his early days Jack Nicklaus was famous for not responding to the crowd's enthusiasm. Videos show a grim determination in his face combined with alertness and great focus. Is this Shakti? Yes, and so is the soft look of communion that other players have when they are perfectly attuned to their game. Each person puts his own stamp on life energy as it flows through. Shakti, although a goddess, isn't the same as a person's feminine side. In both men and women there is a guiding force that shapes life into exactly the activity that is perfectly right for who they are. I once read that in every lifetime there is a high point, a single aspiration or triumph, that the entire lifetime is centered on. We promote as heroes those who cross the Atlantic in solo flight or set an Olympic record because they so obviously achieve what they aspire to. They are more than heroes, however: Such people have harnessed Shakti to achieve a major goal in life. We are all meant to follow Shakti to the core of our selves; we were created to achieve our aspirations rather than simply circle them. We've all touched, however briefly, a place that says, "I am doing exactly what I should be doing at this very moment." At such a moment you are directly connected to your Shakti.

Like the energy harnessed in the stars, Shakti cannot be created or destroyed. It can only be transformed. Your body, in fact, is nothing less than a transformer, a mechanism for taking the energy born at the moment of creation and dispersing it this instant. Your mind can't possibly decide on the literally billions of transformations under way. With your next meal, trillions of new molecules will enter your bloodstream, bearing minuscule packets of chemical energy that must be either stored, combined, suppressed, unleashed, dissipated, or conserved—and the ability to turn this firestorm of raw power into a beautifully ordered structure belongs to Shakti. Without Shakti the sugar that feeds your brain would be the inert sugar in your coffee; without Shakti the oxygen molecules sustaining your heartbeat would be as passive as gas in a balloon.

Shakti combines passion and detachment.

Winning through detachment sounds like a strange concept, one that puts many people off. They automatically equate detachment with indifference or passivity. Yet you must detach from winning in order to win. Some players describe detachment in other terms such as being "centered" or "getting out of your own way." They all come down to disarming the ego. The ego can't help but look outside for validation. It needs victory and feels depleted without it. In all sports there is a world of difference between the roaring crowds and the lonely locker room. Does a spiritual person not care about this? Is it enough just to be at peace within, regardless of how the game turns out? If that were true, no one would play the game. We would all seek out silent retreats and meditate.

Winning can be spiritual, because not just the ego is satisfied. Every experience nourishes the soul. Winning can be sweet or it can be bitter; the difference lies solely in what happens inside. The soul wants sweet experiences, but it learns from bitter ones. As you weave your way between these two poles, you grow spiritually. Once you appreciate the emotional drama being played out, it's no wonder that golf pierces to the soul. At any moment defeat can be snatched from the jaws of victory, yet the most impossible shots can also go right. The whole game is like life condensed to its essence, lightning caught in a bottle.

Matching up ego and soul is one of the major goals of spirituality.

The greatest joy in life comes when inner and outer experiences match each other. Then winning feels like a sublime event. It doesn't fall flat or leave you exhausted. It tastes just the way you dreamed it would. The matchup happens through a process called surrender. As everyone knows, surrender means giving up. In spiritual terms we change this simply to giving. You give of yourself without any selfish desire to take back. I once read that anyone who truly desires to take nothing from others will have the whole universe at his disposal. With this attitude in mind, surrender comes naturally. It isn't necessary to fight against the ego's urge to control, manipulate, and cling.

Consider putting, which has always been the control freak's downfall. Putting puts to the test your ego's claim that it knows how to win. Winning isn't something that can be known. The outcome of any event belongs completely to the unknown. Only when you give up and surrender to the putt does it start pouring into the hole as if drawn by a magnet or a string. Under those magical conditions, even distance doesn't seem to matter. A 30-footer will go in as surely as a 2-footer.

I'm sure you've seen TV shots of impossibly long putts that don't just go in but seem to be drawn in as if by an invisible string. Sometimes this string is all but visible to the player. He will start to stride after the ball, certain that its course is completely true. We all feel the thrill of magic watching these rare moments, and the networks love to show them over and over.

What dawned on me after I went through my own futile attempts to control putts, making the odd 15-footer but never twice in a row, missing too many 2-footers to the point of utter disbelief, was this: If I couldn't control the magic, I could give in to it. So now, after taking my stance and gripping the putter the way I was taught, I take one look at the cup and inside myself I say to the hole, "I'm giving my ball to you."

Only then do I hit it and just let go. I trust that there is always a string tied between the ball and the cup. The string isn't a mystery, it is a form of exact coordination that can be organized only by a higher intelligence. Putting is one of those deep riddles best solved by knowing you can't solve it. When you truly know that, the door of simplicity opens. You perform the necessary setup without worry, repetition, and fuss. (Putts repay overattention by going more wrong than ever, so being simple in your setup doesn't lose anything, no matter where the ball goes.) Then you give yourself to Shakti. And she will step in. They say Shakti is a she because for every god who abides in silence there must be a goddess to dance with him, which is to say that there must be love. It might sound embarrassing to others that I putt with love, but I do. I want the goddess to help me, and being wise, she responds only to love. Surrender flowers here, where there is nothing to fear, nothing to control, nothing to judge. Perhaps you can only give in to the magic 5 percent of the time today, but tomorrow it could be 10 percent.

Shakti doesn't come and go. She is always dancing. She is dancing around the hole coaxing the next putt to go in. What if it doesn't? Your allegiance shouldn't waver. Don't be tempted to employ the endless tweaking that lures so many discouraged golfers. Instead tell yourself, "I asked a goddess to organize this putt the best way possible, and for this moment in my game, the best way possible came true."

Applied to Life

How can you woo Shakti and make her stay with you? For this there is no technique. In various schools of Yoga, years can be spent in disciplined breathing known as Pranayama, whose purpose is to make a fiery energy rush up the spine, an energy known as Shakti. Once it reaches the brain, the fiery energy sets it on fire. Other teachings awaken Shakti through long meditation, leaving almost no time for anything else. And those on the path of the devotee set up altars and worship Shakti, coaxing her presence with offerings of flowers and incense.

I mention this to underscore that Shakti is more elusive than any other aspect of spiritual life. Therefore I believe the simplest way to woo her is through faith. Have faith that you are seen and known and guided by a presence you might never catch with your five senses. This presence has cared for you since before time. It knows what you need to do next; therefore if you substitute faith for other ways of making decisions—ways based on calculation, worry, control, neediness, and ego—the way of Shakti will be there in all its power. I am not being deliberately vague. Surrender is not an action that follows a plan or diagram. Every day you have to let out your faith another inch, saying, "The answer is already here. I am willing to watch it unfold." Having this attitude pays off dividends over time, because the power you are calling on is so immense that it can only be invited in by degrees. As one master wryly said, "I could open up your Shakti in thirty days, but it would take thirty men to hold you down." Be patient. Know that this all-knowing power is real and that it has the intent of pouring through you, making you the expression of the highest aims of spirit. With this attitude, faith forges a link to the miraculous as nothing else can.

LESSON 6

✳

The Ball Knows Everything

The next morning, Adam woke up to find that he was floating above his bed. At first he paid no attention to this miracle, thinking he surely must be asleep. He recalled fuzzily that he had been dreaming he was in the camera tower peering down on the Old Course–St. Andrews during a tournament—a very pleasant sight, although he did pity the players down on the course. They were milling around like ants whose hill has been stepped on. From his bird's-eye view, Adam saw why. Each green had been modified with ten holes instead of one. Tiny angry officials kept scribbling black marks on the scorecard of anyone who sank a ball into the wrong hole, which of course they all did.

That must be frustrating, Adam had thought. He noticed

that he was still floating as the Old Course melted away. In a second he would touch back down on the mattress. But the floating sensation didn't go away. Adam waited a moment more, pondering what to do if he opened his eyes and he actually *was* floating a foot off the mattress. It would change his future considerably. Newspapers would hound him. He would have his pick of TV interviews.

Think they'll ever believe you? That was a sobering thought. Just as Adam decided to keep the miracle private rather than risk public ridicule, the alarm went off on the night table, startling him. Adam reached out to punch the button. To his great disappointment the clock was at the same level it always was. He opened his eyes to confirm that he had landed, then got up with a sigh.

Something persisted, though, after this mirage of a miracle. Brushing his teeth and getting ready for work, Adam kept feeling like he was looking down at himself. He still stared levelly at his face in the bathroom mirror, but the person behind his eyes was somehow above his head, too, like a sparrow on a branch. Adam drove to work without crashing into anything, despite the fact that when he turned his glance this way and that, the part of himself viewing things from above kept looking straight ahead. Not that this made any sense. It just was.

I've split in two, Adam thought at first, but after a few hours he knew he wasn't deluded or distressed. In fact, he went through the day feeling better than ever and ended it almost as fresh as he began despite the usual office tempests and snags. Nothing seemed to get to him. That is, nothing got to *him,* the one looking down. Adam waited for dramatic developments, yet none came. For five days the other Adam simply hung around.

Then he realized that there had been a change. Adam never caught the exact instant when the merging happened. He would be bending over his desk, lost in a welter of details, only to notice that there wasn't two of him but just one. By Friday the other Adam had gone away. Either that or the blending was complete, he couldn't tell which, because there he could still detect the faintest presence of the other Adam.

"I have a twin," he announced to Leela in the shack on Saturday. Adam had waited for half an hour before she entered. The day was cool, September waning into October. Dust had gathered on the floor and windowsills of the shack. Adam wondered why Leela had stopped her meticulous cleaning.

"Does he have a handicap, other than being your twin?" Leela joked.

"I don't think he plays the game," Adam said. "I sort of thought you had something to do with this."

Leela shook her head. She was looking at Adam out of the corner of her eye, as if searching for something no one could spot directly. "You say he just watches?" she asked, her tone growing more interested. "All the time?"

"As far as I can tell," said Adam.

"Hmm." Leela seemed more intrigued than she had ever been before. Finally she came to a conclusion. "You've found something you lost long ago—yourself."

"That seems impossible," said Adam.

"No," Leela insisted, "he's the higher self you forgot that you had."

"I forgot him, even though he's me?" said Adam.

"Right. It's a case of forgetting to remember, or not remembering that you forgot. Take your pick." Listening to herself, she managed a small smile. This remark sounded mystifying, even for her.

"What brought him back, then?" asked Adam, who was fairly certain he was about to get another peculiar answer back. He wasn't disappointed.

"He didn't come back, because he never went away," said Leela. "Without him, the silent witness who is part of every thought and action, you couldn't exist. Yet somehow you lost him. Strange."

"Too strange," Adam mumbled.

"Do you know about the holy fool who went around turning over rocks and looking behind trees?" Leela asked.

"What does that have to do with—"

"Someone asked him what he was doing," Leela went on,

"and the fool said he was looking for his glasses. 'But you're already wearing them,' the bystander mocked. 'Of course,' said the fool, turning over the next rock, 'If I didn't wear them, I'd never find anything.' "

Leela seemed amused by her little parable. Then, as quick as summer lightning, her mood changed. "Everyone has a self they forgot," she said, glancing away from Adam. Even though she was just a young girl dressed, as always, in her white shirt and blue shorts, Adam was certain she saw the world through the same eyes as *she,* the one who witnessed.

"It's amazing how much suffering people have to go through, all for a bit of forgetting," Leela said after a pause.

"Even me?" asked Adam. "I've been trying."

"No," said Leela with affectionate tolerance. "You must have learned your last lesson. Finding your higher self again indicates you are detached. Instead of being swamped by all the stuff that goes on, you made enough space to look for what's really important."

"Oh," said Adam. It was hard to shake the notion that Leela was the one who made everything happen.

"Pretty soon you are going to find yourself turning into that witness. You won't even recognize the old Adam when the new Adam appears," said Leela.

"And I thought this was about my golf game," he said, suddenly uncomfortable.

"It's about The Game," Leela said, adding invisible capitals. "I sort of misled you when we first met. I'm not teaching you anything."

"But you gave me those perfect shots and that magic touch in the dark. You did all those things," Adam protested. Despite the constant encouragement she gave him, he secretly suspected that Leela didn't think much of him. Even the layer of dust that she hadn't bothered to sweep out of the shack seemed like a portent that one day soon she would not return.

"No, you did it all yourself," said Leela. "No one can teach you to master the game, because you already are a master. That's the only way we could have gotten anywhere."

Adam stared at her, a chill running down his spine. Leela's voice carried such finality that he knew he must be near the end of the chase. Yet only Leela knew what they were chasing.

"Your higher self, that's what we've been pursuing all along," said Leela, reading his mind. "It's the only thing you can lose while still having it. It's the only thing you can find without knowing you're looking."

Leela didn't move or make any magical signs in the air, but for a split second Adam saw himself as she did. He saw a master who never doubted, never feared, never went astray. It thought with his mind and touched the world through his senses.

This is the truth, he thought—only he was expanded so far

and high beyond his usual self that it made no sense to call it a thought. It was more like a flicker in the mind of God.

Adam opened his eyes without realizing that he had closed them. "Leela?" he said. Instead of getting a reply, he heard the rickety door clack shut. Unable to fight her restlessness, Leela had walked outside. Adam followed her into the crisp afternoon brightness.

"Leela?"

He found himself alone under the withered oak. Leela didn't leave a trace, not even lingering puffs of dust kicked up by her shoes. Adam, who had been exhilarated a moment before, felt a wave of foreboding.

"Come back, we haven't had our lesson yet!" he shouted into the low wind. But his real fear ran deeper. He feared that if Leela left, his double, the master of the game, would vanish with her.

Driving home on the old dirt road, Adam's unease evaporated. Instead of heading home, he took a sharp turn and wound up at the practice range. Since he was a kid he had often gone there to hit a casual bucket of balls for relaxation or to think. This time he had no motive. It just seemed like something he should do. Despite his doubts, Adam was beginning to feel a new submerged confidence. He no longer believed any impulses were blind. Every impulse was a hint of something to come, a layer of the onion as yet unpeeled, a page of the book ready to be turned.

In a state of heightened alertness he walked over to the line of mats and set down a ball. Adam took his stance, aware that something unusual was about to happen. He swung easily, and the ball rose and sailed, coming to earth at the 150-yard marker. If something exceptional was in the wind, it didn't appear. There was only the slightest tremble in the follow-through, which Adam ignored.

He teed up another ball and hit it. This one rose like the first, sailed a fair distance, and came down near the same marker. In fact, it came down an inch from the first ball. Again there was a slight tremble in Adam's arms during the follow-through.

What is this? he mused. But no voice from the beyond gave him any clues, and without Leela he wondered if he wasn't just wasting time. He hit a third ball, then a fourth. Each shot landed in the same exact place. Adam tried one with his eyes shut. It landed so precisely next to his last shot that the two balls clicked.

He stood back. No one but himself was taking any notice. The only other person hitting balls was a burly man in yellow pants who was too intent on smacking the cover off the ball to look Adam's way. It occurred to Adam that something fantastic was happening, if only he could figure out what it was.

"You're not looking in the right place," said a familiar voice. Adam hadn't seen Leela walk up.

"You're back," said Adam, not bothering to disguise his overwhelming relief. He really had doubted that she would come back.

"You should be noticing something," said Leela, putting down the next ball for him. "Don't bother about where it goes. That's not going to change."

"Okay." She was making him as confused as ever, but Adam accepted it happily. He swung at the ball the same as before. This time, as it sailed inexorably to join the other balls like eggs in a nest, Leela lightly touched his arm at the finish. Again there was a slight tremble, but instead of ignoring it, Adam felt it vibrate longer. The tremble left his arm and went through his body to the ground. He started to tell Leela, but she held a finger to her lips. *Listen.* Adam focused as intently as he could. The tremble kept going, and something incredible happened.

"I moved the world," he whispered.

Leela nodded. "The game wanted you to know. Try again," she said.

The heightened alertness remained with him. He swung at three more balls without a word, and each time the tremble in his arms sent a vibration through the ground that moved the whole world.

Wow. He didn't understand, but he couldn't deny it either.

"That's how it has always been," said Leela. "When you hit the ball, everything shifts. Nothing can be the same ever again. Because of you alone, the game changes. It adds a new dimension."

"Yes," Adam had to agree. "But does it make a difference?"

"Only you can answer that," said Leela. Adam hit another ball, and this time his shot reverberated in all directions. As far as his mind could detect, things changed. Tiny electrons took notice in the nearest star. A supernova flared brighter by a minuscule amount that no one in the universe could possibly notice. But Adam did.

"What does this mean?" he murmured, hardly able to bring his mind back to the little patch of ground where he and Leela were standing.

"It means you know what you're doing," said Leela. "Until you see that every action changes the whole universe, you can't know what you're doing. Not really. You will always be seeing things too small. Now you've seen the truth, which takes in everything."

Adam was listening, but he was elsewhere at the same time. Or maybe one should say he was everywhere. He swung the driver a few more times, letting his mind float out in time and space. For it wasn't just the distant galaxies that trembled when he drove the ball. Past and future were also eavesdropping. Creation was helpless to resist his game.

"What can I do with this?" Adam asked. His feeling of awe was so great that he wasn't even excited.

"You can finally let go," said Leela. "Why do people cling and grab and fight to get their next reward? Because they are afraid of loss. It seems incredibly difficult to cling to your small place in the world. But if you are part of everything, what is there to lose? When you act, the universe sends back a result—the only result that could possibly exist. So that means the entire universe is expressing itself through you, here and now."

Leela didn't give Adam one of her sharp looks. She didn't seem interested in whether he was even paying attention. Instead she rolled a ball out of the bucket and hit a shot, the only one Adam had seen from her since their first meeting. Leela's swing looked almost casual, yet her ball landed 60 yards beyond his.

"You expected mine to land next to yours, didn't you?" Leela laughed. "Don't get too cocky. We're all playing the same game and different games at the same time. You're not the only one changing the universe."

As they stood together as equals and finished off the remaining fifty balls, Adam felt his insecurity fade away. But the bigger change was in the flight of the ball as he hit it. Adam no longer saw his shot as a result. It wasn't a draw or a fade, long or short, right or wrong. Each swing captured the sum total of what the universe was feeling at that very instant. Forces beyond his imagination were funneling into that exact moment, conspiring to make reality what it had to be. Because he was cradled in the womb of the universe, Adam had nothing to worry about. The ball knew his aspirations and his hopes, what he had been and was yet to come. The ball knew everything.

Playing the Game

The sixth lesson is about impeccability. Impeccability literally means being without flaw. In golf, to be impeccable means being able to make any shot you desire. That doesn't happen, yet it is by no means clear why. In a sentence written in the 1920s, Bobby Jones acknowledged that even the best golfers step up to the tee with a sense of insecurity: "It would seem that if a person has hit a golf ball correctly a thousand times, he should be able to duplicate the performance almost at will, but such is certainly not the case."

Life would be impeccable if our desires came true, if each one benefited us, and if they harmed no one and nothing.

Everyone's life moves forward by desire. The start of a golf tournament brings a new spurt of optimism, because in the desire to win each player feels equal. The first tee is like a birth. But then the hitches and glitches appear. In a matter of minutes the course can crush a player's spirits, and the desire to win turns into something much degraded: the desire simply to survive. Everyone has experienced this shift—in the myth of Eden it was called the Fall—but can we ever live without something going wrong? Can we be again without flaw, that is, impeccable?

Not until we solve the mystery of karma. The hitch that intervenes between a desire and its fulfillment is called karma. The word means "action" in Sanskrit. Karma is not random action, however. It is personal action, the kind that moves your life forward or backward. So-called bad karma harms you. It puts up obstacles, slows progress, leads to loss of energy and lack of direction. So-called good karma promotes life energy. It brings about desires as quickly as possible and gives a confident sense of direction. One or the other tendency is always at work. (I am saying "so-called" out of respect for the unpredictable way in which the seemingly bad or good can turn out to have surprisingly different effects when one sees the whole picture.)

When karma makes itself known, it is usually through habits and tendencies that severely limit what is possible. Golfers know this as streaks and slumps. Despite giving the game as much time, energy, desire, and skill this week as they did last, they don't get the same results. Karma has intervened. Or in the middle of a steady game that seems under control, a completely unpredictable disaster occurs. Karma again.

Karma, although considered an infinite mystery, is 99 percent habit. Old conditioning prevents us from perceiving the newness born every day. Being impeccable involves being new at every moment. *Play each game as if for the first time.* You are beginning life over with your next breath, your next word, your next thought.

I realized this in my golf game before I had even hit a shot. I was waiting on the tee watching other foursomes. Quickly I saw who had the incurable slice or hook, who hit the ball timidly and who slammed it with devil-may-care abandon, who walked with an apologetic slump of the shoulders and who strode the links like a battleground. What kind of player would I become? My teaching professional showed up, and we began. She placed my body in correct position, talking me through my first swing. Suddenly I realized that this was a kind of birth. I had never done anything wrong in golf because I had never done anything at all. So there was no reason why my body shouldn't respond perfectly, or as perfectly as was physically within my reach.

I could see before my eyes, on that first day of play, that every swing happens a certain way because of the one that came before. My second drive tried to correct the hook in my first; my third drive tried to correct the flatness in my second; my fourth drive tried to correct the return of the hook. On and on the chain of cause and effect grew, link by link. I was witnessing the accumulation of karma. Yet this process was easy to see only at the beginning. Gradually, invisibly, my tendencies began to take hold. Habits developed. I was much less exact than I imagined I would be, and more impatient. I turned out to be too reckless when in danger, relying on raw boldness in place of strategy. There was no escaping the first rule of karma, which is this: *Whatever you do at this moment changes your whole future.*

In life this rule is often overlooked because everyday actions are so small and existence is so great. Your mind can't isolate which tendencies are going to influence you decisively when you get years down the road. Golf, however, *is* isolated. It is a clean karmic mirror, with the ability to bring out the truth about a person almost immediately. I know of corporations that won't hire a CEO until he is taken out on the golf course to be observed, unbeknownst to him, by a psychologist. This forgivably sneaky ploy is considered far more revealing than any interview. As a mirror to life, golf is one of the most perfect ever devised. When someone speaks in whispers about the mystery of golf, this is what they mean.

Every time you walk onto the course you enact your life drama in miniature. In just one round you can find out how someone handles crisis, how they deal with others, how much value they place on finesse as opposed to brute force, whether they will bend the rules under pressure, and above all, what they really think of themselves.

The ball presents a readout of your karma.

Watch someone on the course who is seething with rage, and what do you notice? Their actions tend to be reckless, intemperate, hasty, overemphatic, abrupt, jerky, tense, out of control, blind, heedless, violent, and vindictive. All of these qualities are related to anger, and despite your best efforts to push them down or deny them, if you play from anger, the results will assume these same qualities.

Reckless: You try the impossible shot or the shot that is beyond your abilities.

Intemperate: Your emotions lead you into the shot instead of cooler judgment.

Hasty: You swing or putt too fast, without being settled.

Overemphatic: You miss the green long and wind up out of bounds.

Abrupt: You chop at the ball.

Jerky: Your arms, hands, shoulders, and hips lose coordination with each other.

Tense: Some part of your body freezes up, leading to some part of your swing freezing up.

Out of control: Your swing becomes totally loose, without mechanics and discipline.

Blind: You lose sight of your objective or even lose your ability to see the ball.

Heedless: You ignore advice.

Violent: You are out to hurt the ball.

Vindictive: You are out for revenge against the ball, the course, other players, or yourself.

This is by no means a complete list, but it's long enough

to show just how subtle and pervasive one influence can be. In contact sports a player driven by cold fury can succeed, but not in golf. Golf is too precise, which is what makes it such an amazing magnifier. The firing of a cluster of neurons in the brain turns into a total body motion, which the club, acting like a giant baseball bat, expands manyfold.

Players are wrong to grumble about mishits and lost shots. There are no mishits. The ball is going exactly where your intention sends it. It can't be blamed if you load your shot with conflicting messages and hidden motives. Don't punish the ball just because it knows everything about you. Accept that everything about you will be magnified. Then you will see that your game is incredibly complex. You can never predict what impulse will surface next, or from what level. At the deepest level you can make shots worthy of a champion, while at another you are a frightened beginner. In you a fierce competitor exists alongside a detached observer. All these qualities are present in every player, but they don't all show up at the same time. The ones being displayed are your karma, the actions that belong to you right this moment.

It's wrong to be fatalistic about karma, as so many people seem to be. Karma merely sets up the situation you find yourself in. It leaves up to you the choice that will resolve that situation. Karma creates the circumstance, not the outcome. How can you get past the obstacles that "bad" karma puts in your way? The answer will seem strange to some. *No matter what you choose, play to be free.* Karma holds a secret, which is that it sticks to you only as long as you need it. If you think you belong in a box, the lid will stay shut. But the moment you don't need to be there, it opens with the slightest touch. In golf, those players with the incurable slice or the inability to sink a clutch putt have made their own traps. They refuse to see that it takes no unusual effort or will to get out. The urge to freedom is incredibly powerful; one only has to act on it.

Look at yourself, feel what is going on, then act.

When you are stuck in a karmic pattern, you are a prisoner of old conditioning. You think you see reality, but in fact you are viewing it through the lens of the past. Most of life consists of trying to break out of patterns that want to hold on tight. Inertia, the tendency to drift along the same old paths, is karma's great ally, and alertness, the tendency to be aware, its great opponent. I am not implying that karma is therefore totally negative. But with experience we all learn that ingrained patterns, whether they feel positive or negative, create a drag on being awake and alert to life in the present moment.

All those players with incurable hooks and slices could break free, yet we find it far easier to keep the old drama going. A few minutes into any round and you know how these dramas work, because they fall into deep, well-worn grooves. The drama of blame, the drama of control, the drama of the victim, the drama of passive acceptance. None of these will lead to freedom; their only reason for existence is to perpetuate themselves, because only by convincing you to behave a certain way can the voices of blame, control, manipulation, and withdrawal survive.

Once you see that a tendency is harming you, what next?

Without a guiding vision, freedom would be pointless. It would be nothing more than an intuition to be lost and drifting, which we certainly see on all sides. The great spiritual masters, realizing this, advised every person to live with one ultimate goal in mind: *unity.* Unity means that you have joined your higher self. In this marriage there are no gaps or separations. You know exactly what is needed at any given moment. Instead of using your small individual mind to calculate what you should do, you allow the cosmic mind to decide for you.

When you stop attaching yourself to your actions, impeccability emerges.

When you reach unity you will be impeccable. Actions that bring you closer to unity are known as Karma Yoga, from the root Sanskrit words for action and union. There are long lists of how to behave on the way to unity, including giving, trusting, loving, doing no harm, thinking virtuously, and obeying only life-enhancing impulses. But to me Karma

Yoga comes down to one thing: Act from that place inside you that is already free. When you have a choice to make, allow your initial reactions to settle. Notice your usual tendency, whatever it is, and then set it aside. Say no to anger, blame, control, manipulation, passivity, victimization, and withdrawal. This is asking a lot, but any tendency, no matter how well it has worked in the past, ties you tighter to karma.

Having stepped aside, ask for the right response, the one that would benefit everyone concerned. Then listen for what comes to you from the place of freedom, your higher self. How will you know when it speaks? The higher self never has a voice. It is always silent, a knowing without words that immediately propels you into action. Every other voice, whether it sounds good or bad, is from the past. Even the saintliest words are messages from ego.

What if the pure, simple action doesn't arise? Move on. You have done your best for now. A thousand other choices are waiting in the wings. The crux of the matter is this: The more you ask for guidance, the more you will know it when it comes. There is always a silent communication between you and your higher self. It sends you messages from its place of freedom, and you receive them in your position of bondage. Little by little, the messages become clearer. Year by year, you understand more of the truth from your higher self. You discover that you were born to achieve freedom because it is already yours. When that happens, you have no choice but to do what is best for you. From the place of bondage you slip silently into the place of utter freedom. This is the true arrival of grace.

Applied to Life

Achieving impeccability is the same as reaching enlightenment, therefore it is a lifelong pursuit. Any technique to make the journey easier would have to be workable every day, every hour, every minute. It would have to be your lifelong companion yet closer than any spouse or lover, because this is an intimacy of the self with the self.

I can imagine only one such technique, and that is to pay attention. The phrase sounds harmless; it's usually employed in a nagging, negative way: "You're not paying attention to me." But attention is awareness of who you are, where you are, and what is going on, all at once. Someone who is impeccable doesn't have to be smarter or stronger than anyone else. All that's needed is not to have lapses of attention. Your antennae have to be out all the time—or rather, *in* all the time, because attention is an inward gift.

It sounds exhausting to be awake all the time. The mind needs to sleep as does the body. Yet being awake is just the closest approximation of the real thing. Attention doesn't mean being on your toes twenty-four hours a day like a military guard at his post. Attention is actually just flexibility—

knowing when to rest and when to strike, when to reach out and when to go inward, when to speak and when to be in silence.

Will you have to train to become this acute at every moment? I don't believe so. Although in the East recluses spend a lifetime trying to discipline their attention, what impeccability brings is spontaneity. To be completely flexible, you have to be willing to turn on a dime. The path to impeccability can be followed today and always:

* Be willing to redefine yourself every day.

* Watch yourself falling into old habits and beliefs, then stop as soon as you catch yourself.

* Accept total responsibility for every response and feeling you have. Do not cast them out onto anything or anyone external to you.

* Take the world to be a true mirror of who you are at this very instant.

* Receive whatever is trying to come in. Messages are every-where. Your next step doesn't have to be thought out. It will simply appear before you at the right time.

* Don't act when you are in doubt. Don't make decisions when you are uncertain. Practice patience until you know for sure.

* Assume that God has His total attention on you.

These are not techniques but states of mind, and if you write them down and look at them regularly, they can become as ingrained in you as any habit—for impeccability is first a habit, then an instinct, and finally a spontaneous way of living in the world that needs no reminder because the path opens up as freely as tomorrow's dawn.

LESSON 7

✳

Let the Game Play You

✴ Leela had warned Adam not to get too cocky, but how could he not? Over the next week he kept his clubs in the trunk of his car, and the moment he could break free from the office, he raced out to play. He hit buckets of balls in the rain and joined any group he could find at the country club. Every free moment allowed him a chance to marvel at what he'd become. A master. Leela had not told him he was a master. She didn't have to, just as she didn't have to announce that there would be no more lessons. Adam's whole body told him, and so did his mind.

In his fantasy he envisioned the television crews covering his victory march to the last hole at the Masters while commentators scrambled to discover who this unknown amateur was, this brilliant phenom who had achieved the impossible when he broke 20 under par for the tournament.

Adam almost trembled when he teed up a ball because he knew his next shot would be amazing. Anyone who had ever played with him before he knew Leela would have been dumbfounded. His long drives were fired from a cannon; his putts 25 feet out found the hole like a billiard ball on a felt-top table.

But Adam didn't let anyone from the old days see him. He couldn't imagine explaining how he had risen to his new glory. He preferred pickup games with strangers who assumed that he was a very, very good player dropping by to show them how it was done.

"Are you a professional?" a dentist asked one afternoon after Adam holed a bunker shot from 60 feet and a down-hill lie. (The fact that he had even landed in the sand must have been a whim of the golf gods, just to show him what he could do.)

"No, not yet," Adam said enigmatically. He liked walking around with an air of mystery. He only regretted that Leela wasn't there to see what she had created.

A week turned into a month, and by the end of November the trees had shed their leaves around the course. The groundskeepers were bustling to put the greens to bed for the winter; the rough was being let go and had grown up to

Adam's knees in some spots. Sometimes he stayed on the course so late that the whippoorwills sang their twilight song and foraging quail dotted the dim fairways. But still Adam kept on playing—he would have played in the snow if they let him—because once he stopped he didn't quite know if the spell would be broken forever.

The day before Thanksgiving was a beauty, with open skies and a sun so bright it gave the illusion of being warm outside. Adam skipped breakfast to show up at eight for his tee-time—no one would be at the office, anyway. The first tee was empty. Rather than waiting for a group to gather, he played alone until he reached the ninth tee. Looking up, Adam saw the sun disappear in a haze of low-lying clouds. A raw wind cut in from the north, and for a moment, standing there on the edge of winter, Adam considered turning back. Then the thought passed, and he hit his drive off the tee. It felt good (didn't all his shots feel good?), yet bizarrely the ball veered in midair as if swatted by an invisible hand and came to earth deep in the left rough.

What? Adam was reluctant to believe where the ball had gone. He trudged into the tall grass and took a hasty swipe at it. He expected the shot to be choppy because of the deep lie, but instead nothing happened at all. He had whiffed completely. The second try was another whiff that had so much anger behind it his whole body whirled around.

This is impossible.

Adam barely had time to think these words before he felt beads of panic sweat under his scalp. He looked around. The raw wind cut through his clothes as if they were mosquito netting, and he trembled from head to foot. But it wasn't the cold. He realized that exactly this same series of shots had taken place last August, on the day he had started his pilgrim's progress.

The next shot, he knew, would zig crazily across the fairway into the woods. Adam backed away from his stance, feeling sick. This time around there was no foursome on the tee laughing at him and no smirking teenage caddie to run after the ball. Those details didn't matter. Adam imagined the worst—that this had all been a dream that was starting to unravel the same way it had begun. But he had no choice except to take his shot.

He planted his feet carefully and did everything he had been taught. The ball filled his field of vision. He imagined a line connecting his heart to the ball. He swung without haste and let the swing be what it needed to be. To no avail. The ball jumped up like a wounded bird and flew off into the deep woods. It was all coming apart, and there was nothing he could do about it.

Because the leaves had fallen, he didn't have to hack his way through the underbrush as much as before, and there was no cold rain dripping down his neck from the tall, gloomy pines.

"Where are you?" Adam said aloud. He was talking to his lost ball, but also to the man he knew would be there.

"Having trouble?" a voice said, but it wasn't the resonant voice of the mysterious stranger.

"Leela!" Adam cried. And there she was, standing beside him when he was sure no one had been there the moment before. Adam had grown so used to her that he hadn't realized how sad it had made him to lose her.

"Here we are again," she said. For the first time, she wasn't dressed for golf. In place of the blue shorts and white shirt, she was wrapped in a long gray cape. Adam shivered.

"I need more lessons," Adam said. "My game fell apart without you."

"No, it didn't," said Leela. "This is your game now. Let's find your ball. I think you'll be lying five after going out of bounds. No, six."

"Wait," said Adam, feeling his heart sink. "My game? No, this is the game I started with. It's a mess! Don't take it all away," Adam said. He was trying hard not to plead, but he couldn't go back to what he'd been. He couldn't lose everything.

"You think you've mastered the game?" asked Leela. "You just had a bag of great shots."

"Which I get to keep?" said Adam anxiously.

Leela ignored his appeal. "If all you have is a bag of great shots, you don't have anything. Not until you take the last step."

"Which is what?" asked Adam.

"The last step is mystical," said Leela, cocking her head like a quizzical bird. Adam almost laughed. *Mystical?* The word sounded so peculiar coming from her. He had long ago stopped thinking of Leela as merely human; he even had a suspicion that she might be the stranger who had first met him in the dark woods, transformed by the magic cloak that all but swallowed up her small body.

Leela quickly went on. "How can you tell when a shot is good or bad?" she asked. "Imagine that a few months ago you'd hit a perfect tee shot on this hole and had never met me. Would that have been a good shot? Or what about a shot you shank 30 feet into the rough, only to find that the next player a hundred yards ahead is hit by lightning. It could have been you. Is that still a bad shot?"

Because Leela took a long time to say all this, and because her voice was soft and soothing, Adam began to feel less afraid. She noticed and nodded. "When you take the last step," said Leela, "a good shot and a bad shot are the same."

"That's impossible," Adam blurted out. "If that was true, there would be no point to the game."

"I hear that a lot," Leela remarked. She stooped to pick

something up from the ground. "Take it," she said, handing Adam back his ball, which had rolled almost out of sight under a pile of leaves.

Reluctantly Adam took the ball and began to thrust it back into his pocket when something caught his attention. Dimples. The textured surface of the ball was indented all over. It was a familiar texture, one he'd always loved. At first Adam assumed that he noticed the dimples for no particular reason or just because the feel of the ball was reassuring, a solid thing he could hold on to. But there was something else. Under his touch the dimples were different. In each one he could feel a moment of his life, and at every moment there had been a choice.

Yes or no? This or that? Right or wrong?

"Too many to count," Leela murmured. "You think you can figure out every one?"

Adam couldn't reply, because the texture of the ball kept fascinating him. He rolled it under his fingers some more.

"Pick a moment," Leela whispered.

Adam's mind flashed back to the moment when he was lying awake in bed, wondering whether to go to the shack for the first time.

"Good," Leela whispered. "What do you see?"

Adam saw himself lying in bed, wondering what choice to make. Should he go to the old highway? What would happen? Was it a trick? As he felt the ball, each dimple posed a new question, and no matter how hard he tried to stop his mind, the questions multiplied. There were a hundred reasons to meet his destiny at the shack where Leela would be waiting, but a hundred others not to go. His whole life stretched ahead like a road whose every turning changed with each possibility.

"Pick a possibility," Leela whispered.

Fascinated, Adam rolled the ball in his hand again. He saw himself standing at the end of the dirt road. It was a dead end. There was no shack. There was no magic door to open. Resentfully he turned his dusty car around and went home.

"You look unhappy," Leela said. "You wouldn't want to lose her, would you?"

I am losing her, Adam thought. The next moment it struck him how strange it was that they both referred to Leela as if she were someone else.

"Look around," Leela said. Adam noticed now that they were standing in a dense fog that had crept over the woods. "See this?" said Leela. Adam nodded. "No, I mean do you really see it?" Leela said urgently.

Adam raised his face and lifted it against the fog, taking it in. Then he saw and he knew. The fog was what he had been living in all his life. Too many moments, too many choices, too many possibilities to figure out. They swirled around him.

"Everyone faces too many moments and choices and possibilities," said Leela. "You can keep living that way. Or you can get out of the fog."

"How?" said Adam.

"You know, very few people ask that question," said Leela, looking pleased for the first time that day. "The fog is endless and oddly comforting. It's the spell we are afraid to break."

Adam dropped the ball, unable to touch it anymore.

"Pick it up," Leela said. "Feel what comes next." Adam backed away as if the ball were a grenade. "It won't bite you," she said. "It's just a ball."

Adam knew better. "If I do, it will be the last step. I won't ever go back."

"Well, of course," Leela laughed. "Why do you think the game is worth playing?"

"I can't," Adam said in a hoarse voice.

"I know," said Leela, softening her tone. "No one can. It's a very old story."

Leela bent over and picked up the ball. Before Adam could react, it plopped into his palm, and he felt Leela cup their hands together, so that the two held the small white sphere in one grip.

"Feel it again," she whispered. "Feel the unknown."

Adam trembled. The dimples were infinitesimal now. They were like sand, then like the dust of creation sifting through his fingers. He tried to hold on tight, but the precious motes streamed out of his grasp. He would have gotten down on his knees to sweep them up, but they never ended. A fine, sparkling dust flowed and flowed around him, unending, inexhaustible. It created world after world and then burst them like bubbles. Creation was destruction at the same time, light married to dark, eternity spinning to the music of time.

Now Adam knew why no one had ever taken the last step alone. Because God had to come with us. Only in God can everything be born, live, and die all at once. For a split second Adam could see with God's eyes. The ball disappeared in his grasp, and as it did, his hand disappeared with it, then his arm, and up to his body. His blood and bones melted into emptiness, his thoughts dissolved, and the only thing left was the faintest spark, a spark of life that floated like a leaf in the wind. He was as carefree as a leaf, but he was the wind also and therefore could never be lost or alone. This ineffable sensation told him something.

I am.

Then it was over.

"Amazing, isn't it?" Leela said.

Adam couldn't speak. One second he had been perched on the brink of infinity, the next he was standing in the mud holding a little white ball. But what had happened filled him with a shimmering glow. "Does everyone get to see that?" he murmured.

✳

"Yes, eventually," said Leela. "Today just happened to be your day."

"My day," Adam mumbled. He looked around, and his hand carelessly wiped the back of his neck. It came away wet with rain. The sun felt too hot to be November. He suddenly knew he was back on the day he'd started.

"I think your foursome is waiting," said Leela.

The woods, though thick, were shallow, and Adam could hear his friends shouting for him not a hundred feet away. "I get the feeling I'm not going to win the Open," he said.

Leela shrugged. "Maybe if you practice a hundred thousand hours. You're kind of old to start."

Adam felt a wave of sick disappointment. The great shots were gone forever. Leela would be like a dream that leaves behind only memories too strange to share. "Will I get anything out of this?" he blurted out.

"You've gotten everything there is," said Leela, turning to depart. "Enjoy."

In the blink of an eye, she was lost in the shadows of the pines. Adam trudged back to the fairway. The heavy, damp air of summer fell on his shoulders. When he put his ball down, lying five on the ninth hole—or was it six?—he didn't want to swing at it.

Will I be a loser again?

Adam sighed and pushed the idea from his mind. His foursome was waiting impatiently up ahead. He took his stance and started the club back. He could feel the club go off-plane, and he was out of position at the top. At impact there was nothing like the sharp crack there should have been. Compared to his two whiffs, however, this shot at least didn't humiliate him. It flew a good 150 yards and stayed within bounds.

"Not bad," someone shouted from the tee. There was a small outbreak of laughter.

Not bad at all. Adam turned and gave a faint nod to acknowledge the onlookers. What none could see was the wonder inside him. Adam hadn't hit the ball at all. He hadn't even moved. He was a still point through which, at that very instant, the universe exerted a tiny push. Yet in that push he felt the gush of life pouring forth, eager to be in the world. Life wanted nothing more than to be born at that moment through him.

I am, the universe told him with infinite gratitude.

I am, said Adam in return. There was no more fog. In taking the last step, he was beyond good shots or even great ones.

Adam picked up his bag and started to walk briskly down the fairway so that the group behind could tee off. A lot of people wanted to play the game that day. Only one man on the course wanted something else. He wanted to see how the *game* would play *him.* Adam never spoke of this to anyone, yet it remained the guiding desire of his life from that day on.

✳

Playing the Game

The seventh lesson is about enlightenment. Enlightenment is difficult to speak about and even harder, it would seem, to practice. To the ancient sages it meant *Moksha,* or liberation. No matter how brilliant your mind or advanced your skill, you could not call yourself enlightened unless you were free. The wisest people have looked at life, for all its joys, as a net, and like all nets it has holes. Find a hole and jump through. Then you will have Moksha.

To add to the mystery of all this, the net is invisible. You cannot escape its twists of fate, and even when you are a master, your triumphs will be marred by struggle and sometimes defeat. Yet golf is a contained sport, so it gives you a chance to pick a strategy, and if you pick the right one, it might work in life as well.

Pursuing enlightenment is the strategy that sets you free. Every other strategy, if it succeeds, will only lower your score. Enlightenment focuses entirely on making the self your trusted ally. What happens to your score is left to the unknown (which is not like giving up on your score—the unknown can accomplish anything). This is how I believe the greatest spiritual masters approach life, and if they played golf, their strategy would be the same. A person who is free has no need to focus on outcomes. He is not tied to the opinion of others. He never forces anything, not the smallest action. He refuses to listen to fear. In other words, he lets the game play him instead of the other way around. This strategy works only if you and the game are one; otherwise, the game will toss you up and down like a leaf. You have to become the leaf and the wind at the same time.

To a born competitor, this sounds unbelievable. It undermines his whole rationale for being on the field of play, which is to dominate, to win. Yet that strategy turns the game into a war, and in any war there is always suffering. The Bhagavad Gita suggests that we can step once and for all out of conflict. It says that to a yogi, gain and loss are the same. Is this possible in golf? Can a bad shot and a good one bring equal joy? Absolutely, if what you want out of the game is liberation.

Everyone, not just born competitors, feels a strong urge to reject the notion that loss and gain are the same. So consider it in emotional terms. What if you could play every round of golf with equal commitment? What if you could leave the course as energized and happy as you entered it? That's what freedom feels like. If you experience strain, struggle, pain, anger, and frustration, that's what not being free feels like. Somehow getting free has been turned into serious business. It shouldn't, because a game is different from work. When you play, just showing up is enjoyable. You are under the sun without a care in the world. The perfectly clipped greens and groomed lushness creates a paradise for play, a garden. Something special is meant to happen. Or more than special.

"I had entered a qualifying tournament in Houston for the Open," a longtime player told me. "On a par 5 I reached the green in two. Theoretically I had a shot at eagle, but my ball landed a hundred feet away from the hole on the back tier, with a drop and then a huge break. Realistically I had no chance. But as I stood over the putt, I happened to look up, and I saw a faint rainbow in the sky, just a bit of an arc following a sun shower. At that instant my feet felt as if they merged with the ground. I was actually one with the earth. And I knew with total certainty that I would make the putt. I made my stroke, and the ball landed 15 feet to the left and came back again. No one could have planned such a crazy path, but the ball went right into the hole. Maybe two or three times in my life I've had that same feeling of being one with the earth, and every time it happened, I made the shot."

This was a moment of sheer freedom. No single element came into play; they all did. If you can step outside the complexity of the game, you will transcend your limitations. There's the secret, the hidden key. When you can laugh at a bad shot, you've transcended sorrow. When you can take genuine pleasure in someone else's victory, you've transcended jealousy. When you can feel satisfied with a round of ninety-seven instead of eighty, you've transcended self-importance. Is that really possible in any endeavor? I have a friend who plays chess on the Internet, and when he made a decision, just once, to play a game for the sheer beauty of it, he lost. And he got more frustrated, and he had to fight the self-criticism rising to mock his efforts. The point is not that he could have found an easy way. The point is that only when you set your sights to go beyond outcome can you allow in the possibility of defeating the voice of self-criticism and ending the frustration that holds in check deeper, darker fears.

In its soul, golf is a way to transcend.

Transcendence sounds as heavy and serious as all the rest of the business that spirituality has turned into. But in reality you transcend when you find a way to play, to be free instead of hemmed in. The ancient Indian sages looked past the physical world entirely. They said that if you break down a tree or a rock into its invisible building blocks, you arrive at the same forces that built a star, an angry word, a muscle fiber and a heart cell, a mountain and a poem. These primal forces are forever at play. Creation builds and then decay sets in. Good pushes one way and evil pushes back. Light encroaches on darkness and then darkness sneaks back to reclaim its ground. Seeing this undeniable fact, one has only two choices: Either conquer these primal forces or transcend them.

We've boiled golf down to the same choice posed thousands of years ago when very wise people set out to find a strategy for living. Either you fight or you let the game play you. No one can stop the primordial forces in their fathomless weaving and interweaving. I was intrigued to read an old golf manual from the turn of the century that tried to make the game totally rational. The writer pointed out that everyone has a different swing. In his opinion, trying to force your peculiarities into a "model" swing, one that is cut-and-dried for every player, was hopeless.

He felt there was another way, and he offered this brilliant solution. A perfect swing, he said, only has to be perfect when you hit the ball. For 2 inches in front of contact and 2 inches after, the club face has to be in perfect alignment. This tiny interval is what the whole swing is about. Who cares what the rest looks like? The backswing and the follow-through can be anything they want to be, so long as for a mere 4 inches and the time span lasting a hundredth of a second you line up exactly straight and true.

It was a brilliant idea in its way. If you could control what happens in that tiny interval, you would have a perfect swing. Unfortunately, a player's whole being goes into every shot. Past and present merge in this vital, tense instant; the future will be forever altered by the outcome. Even if a machine could show you precisely what your club was doing a millionth of a second before it struck the ball, you wouldn't be able to escape the vast complexity of the game. Golf really and truly is about facing the unknown, because when you are forced to take in every particle of who you are, it is more than you can ever know.

❋

When you transcend you don't walk away from the game or float above it. You merge. You and the game become one. In that state of complete unity you become free. Nothing opposes you. You can relax and let the game play you, like a child being carried to the end of the journey in his mother's arms.

Once you feel totally secure and safe, other qualities blossom. Compassion, caring, devotion, love. None can be fully expressed when you are caught up in conflict, but in freedom they come naturally. It is not possible to force the feeling of love, to try and love yourself or another because you know you should. Force kills love, just as it kills the game of golf. So an enlightened strategy is based on three promises you make to yourself:

I will never force or strain.
I will go where my joy leads me.
I will allow myself to be who I am.

These are profound promises, because they put us up against huge forces that add strain to our lives, that push us away from joy, that ask us to be who we are not. To win freedom, you must act as if you are free already. In the eyes of the soul you are, so this isn't pretending; this is showing yourself that you know the truth. The enlightened player lets opposites perform their dance. While fully engaging yourself, you don't allow any outcome to damage who you are. Of course, at the level they rule, the forces of nature will throw you around. A whiff isn't the same as a hole in one. The enlightened player finds a place to stand where ups and downs don't throw him around. Such a place can only exist inside.

Let your vision be your game. No one knows what lies ahead, not just in the far future, but ahead as close as the next thought, the next reaction from others, the next loss or gain. The enlightened player is devoted to the unknown, because he understands that this is *what is*. Uncertainty arouses joy instead of dread once you embrace the mystery. A famous physicist from early in the twentieth century, Sir Arthur Eddington, remarked that after a lifetime of studying the cosmos, he knew only one thing: "Something unknown is doing we don't know what."

When you transcend the game, you rejoice in its uncertainty.

There is infinite wisdom in the unfathomable way that life is shaping each of us. The forces of nature pull the world apart like taffy, molding the clay of chaos. But the inner person is immune to chaos; you are being guided toward an end of unutterable beauty and harmony. It takes trust to believe that this is so. In your vision you must see yourself as belonging in Eden, a child of grace and innocence. We all fall short of our vision every day, every hour. But when you have a vision to guide you, rising and falling seem to matter less.

Every wisdom tradition contains the concept of grace.

Grace is the condition closest to God. We instantly recognize who is playing the game gracefully and who is grinding it out instead. But we sometimes mistakenly assume that graceful people are simply born that way. If you define grace as inner harmony, as being close to your soul, then it must be won. At any given moment you can decide to express certain possibilities inherent in everyone, which need nurturing if you really want them to flower. Let me put these in terms of golf.

Finesse: This is a mysterious quality expressed through easy, natural, economical movement. A golfer who has finesse makes the swing look simple. He feels at ease with his body. Externally there is no fighting with the ball, the equipment, or the course.

Dedication: This quality shows serious purpose. Whatever you are dedicated to you take to be important, not for what you can get out of it but for what it is. A dedicated golfer doesn't turn the game into a display of ego. He isn't out to pit his abilities against other players or some imagined score.

Devotion: This quality is dedication carried to the point of reverence. Devotion is loving humility. It puts you beyond the humiliations and triumph of ego. Every twist and turn is cause for appreciation when you are devoted to your game.

Love: This quality has to do with giving. Only to those we love do we truly give ourselves. We are glad to be vulnerable with someone who loves us, because in our openness we actually feel safer than when we are defended. Someone who loves the game touches the essence of the last lesson: Let the game play you.

Best of all, you can step onto the fresh turf of a golf course and for a few hours actually play with the grace that should infuse everything. I recently saw a twelve-year-old girl hitting a bucket of balls on the driving range. She had no swing at all, yet every shot made her smile, and she could barely wait to tee up the next ball before the previous one landed. I watched her for a while, and then I had a flash of what the perfect golf shot would be: to hit the ball and have it never land at all. It would just disappear into eternity. That's the shot she must have been aiming for. In some deep recess we all want that shot. It is the one that sets us free.

EPILOGUE

Leela

✴ Adam never found the hundred thousand hours it would have taken for him to win the U.S. Open. He never earned the green jacket at Augusta or even turned pro. He did become a very, very good golfer. Even better, he got closer every day to accepting a whiff with the same appreciation as a hole in one.

But as he feared, when Leela left there was no one he could share his memories with. Once in a while he would hear somebody waxing eloquent about the game—golf tempts many people that way—and when they got to the stage where it came naturally to say that golf is a lot like life, he wanted to add, "Sure, but if you really get down to it, life is a lot like golf." In his reflective moments he boiled all of Leela's lessons down to that.

Why would it take a divine teacher, an angel or goddess, to show him that? Because on the surface you wouldn't guess that life is a game. It often seems to be an incredibly difficult struggle, and even when it goes well, life doesn't have golf's clear-cut rules, its elegant shape, or its reassuring line between the fairway and out of bounds. Yet each person has to find a strategy for living. Leela's approach to golf suggests that life can be lived from the level of spirit. She taught Adam *what is,* and if you align yourself with *what is,* life can be mastered.

1. *Be of one mind:* The first lesson says that life is woven into wholeness. Everything you see around you expresses a different face of the same unity. This lesson comes first because it states what the whole game is about, which is getting beyond separation. When you are separate, you miss the unity, and therefore you must learn how to find it again.

2. *Let the swing happen:* In separation you don't feel that spirit is supporting you, so you are left to struggle. The more dedicated you are to the struggle, the deeper you dig yourself into separation. The way out is to gradually

allow some part of your daily life to be given over to God (or the universe, if that term is more comfortable). At every level, life is capable of running itself without interference. You have to test that notion before it can come true for you personally.

3. *Find the now and you'll find the shot:* Spirit operates in the present moment. When the Bible says, "Seek and you will find, knock and the door will open," the door in question is now. Reliving the past or anticipating the future are both futile. They keep you in separation by taking you out of the place where spirit waits. Help and healing are in the now.

4. *Play from your heart to the hole:* Your mind can figure out how to solve problems, but there is a more efficient way. Have a desire in your heart, and then release it to spirit. This technique, which has emerged in every wisdom tradition, is the hardest for modern people to practice. But if given a chance, it works. There is an unbroken connection between what you desire and its outcome. In separation we break that thread; in unity we tie it back together.

5. *Winning is passion with detachment:* Spirit doesn't solve life's problems like a servant cutting the lawn while you

sleep in the hammock. You still have to throw yourself into life's challenges with commitment and dedication. Yet at the same time keep in mind that it isn't you that is making anything happen. You are the silent witness, the observer at the center of activity.

6. *The ball knows everything:* It takes a lifetime to completely trust that there is a higher intelligence that can take care of absolutely everything. Mistrust will make you rush in to try and control outcomes. Often you'll succeed, but in the process you will be stepping back from your true goal, which is to get out of separation. It helps to remember that spirit isn't here one day and gone the next. It is present in everything; therefore it knows what to do at all times.

7. *Let the game play you:* In the final lesson the toughest part of life becomes incredibly easy. The toughest part is letting go of all need to control. The temptation always arises to say that you know better than God. But if you are God—that is, if you are spirit—then how can you know better than yourself? Freedom comes when you see the built-in contradiction of trying to manipulate something that is going right to begin with. This is what spiritual masters mean when they say, each in their own way, "Stop trying to steer the river."

Adam was lucky. Not that Leela came to him, because no one is lucky in that regard. When you are ready, the universe always brings you what you need to know. Adam was lucky to fall in love.

It was no secret to him that he loved Leela, despite their difference in age (and despite the fact that, as he suspected, she also took shape as the mysterious man who first met him in the woods).

Love is the kindest teacher and the only one that can melt the mind's resistance. It could have taken Adam many years to learn even one of these seven lessons, but his ego, with all its stubborn habits and conditioning, was no match for love. At night I imagine Adam often dreamed of her. Whether she came as angel or goddess, Leela was *leela,* the divine play itself. She had charmed Adam, reminding him with every smile and tossed-off shrug that it is possible to live with laughter in your heart. In fact, this is the most valuable gift of all and the hardest, in the midst of so much stress, to win. The roles we play bring waves of pleasure and pain that toss us around like corks on the sea. You can only laugh when you see that no role is really you. Roles exist so that spirit can take shape; you are that spirit, outlasting all shapes and all forms. You will be here long after one self-image dissolves to allow spirit to fill another.

In Adam's dreams, Leela never looked the same way twice. She kept changing, because *leela* is a shape-shifter. But he cherished her for who she really was, and one night she came to whisper the secret of immortality in his ear: "Dreams come and go, but the dreamer lives on."

Until we hear that whisper, you and I will never find the Garden of Eden again. Golf gives us a chance. The crack of the club face against the ball knocks at the door of the garden, the whoosh of its flight is our journey back to our blessed beginning, and the swirling drop into the hole is, for the briefest instant, paradise regained. I can imagine other activities that might contribute more to the practical affairs of life but none that so perfectly mirrors our dreams.

About the Author

DEEPAK CHOPRA has written thirty-one books, which have been translated into more than thirty-five languages, including the *New York Times* bestsellers *How to Know God*; *Ageless Body, Timeless Mind*; *Perfect Health*; and *The Seven Spiritual Laws of Success*. He is widely considered a pioneer in the area of mind-body medicine, and speaks to many thousands of people a year about issues concerning the body, mind, and spirit. He has been named one of the Top 100 Icons and Heroes of the Century by *Time* magazine and is the founder of the renowned Chopra Center for Well Being.

For more information on the Golf for Enlightenment Program that is offered by Deepak Chopra and the world-famous golf instructor Mitchell Spearman, please visit www.chopra.com or send an e-mail to golf@chopra.com.

Deepak Chopra and The Chopra Center for Well Being at La Costa Resort and Spa, Carlsbad, California, offer a wide range of seminars, products and educational programmes, worldwide. The Chopra Center offers revitalizing mind/body programmes, as well as day spa services. Guests can come to rejuvenate, expand knowledge or obtain a medical consultation.

For information on meditation classes, health and well-being courses, instructor certification programmes, or local classes in your area, contact The Chopra Center for Well Being at La Costa Resort and Spa, 7321 Estrella Del Mar Road, Carlsbad, CA 92009-6725, USA. By telephone: 001-888-424-6772, or 001-760-931-7509. For a virtual tour of the Center, visit the Internet website at www.chopra.com.

If you live in Europe and would like more information on workshops, lectures or other programmes about Dr. Deepak Chopra or to order any of his books, tapes or products, please contact: Contours, 44 Fordbridge Road, Ashford, Middlesex, TW15 2SJ (tel: +44 (0) 208 564 7033; fax +44 (0) 208 897 3807; email: sales@infinite-contours.co.uk; website: www.infinite-contours.co.uk).

If you live in Australia and would like more information on workshops, lectures, or programmes presented by Dr. Deepak

Chopra, please contact What's On The Planet Pty Ltd, PO Box 161, Brighton Le Sands, NSW 2216, Australia, or email deepak@theplanet.com.au.

Rider books are available from all good bookshops or by ordering direct on 01624 677237. Or visit our website at www.randomhouse.co.uk.